Inside Justice

Inside Justice

Secrets Your Local Court
& Police Don't Want You to Know

M. J. Miczak

Writers Club Press
San Jose New York Lincoln Shanghai

Inside Justice
Secrets Your Local Court & Police Don't Want You to Know

Writers Club Press
an imprint of iUniverse.com, Inc.

For information address:
iUniverse.com, Inc.
620 North 48th Street
Suite 201
Lincoln, NE 68504-3467
www.iuniverse.com

This book is not designed to be a substitute for qualified
and licensed legal advice. The ideas contained herein are personal
examples and experiences only. For any legal issue, you may find a
qualified attorney through your local state Bar Association licensed
to practice law in your state. Once again, always consult with your
attorney before making any legal decisions, transactions or agreements.

ISBN: 0-595-12086-5

Printed in the United States of America

Dedication

"This book is dedicated to the memory of the Hon. James M. Newman"

Table Of Contents

Forward

The events in this book are absolutely true, every word as they occurred to me, the first hand witness. The names have been changed to protect the innocent, (and perhaps even a few guilty ones at that), but the story is totally authentic. It's not important that you know the exact names of the players in this soap opera. What is important is that you understand the concepts upon which the book is based. Those being that no matter where you live in the United States, no matter what state or territory, you have both Constitutional and Civil Rights.

Under these provisions you have special protections that you may not even be aware of. Believe me, very few of those occupying positions of power are ever going to apprise you of them either. That's how they maintain their power, after all! The Bible, the classic read for every civilized person, puts it succinctly when it makes the observation that "Man has dominated man to his ruin." It also goes on to add that "When the wicked rule the people sigh." It's not speaking about a "sigh" of relief either. This sighing is that of oppression, burden and pain. In many ways that sums up the present times we are living in. Politicians and bureaucrats are often concerned with what will benefit them, not the people whom they serve.

Understanding that, you will see that going into today's court room and dealing with local police can be a tricky gambit to run. If you are not aware of your rights, serious advantage can be taken of you as a result. Remember the old saying, "Power corrupts but absolute power corrupts absolutely"? It is very true and those accustomed to enjoying such total control over the lives of others are not likely to relinquish it and many times abuse it.

Hence you need to be on your toes when you are in the court room or in the presence of the police. Otherwise you may find yourself forfeiting your rights to privacy, freedom and perhaps even some hard earned cash. *"Inside Justice..Secrets Your Local Court & Police Don't Want You to Know"* provides a satirical look at some of the most pompous, but true to life characters you'll ever want to meet, (o.k. or maybe not).

Keep in mind that this could be *your* town judge, *your* court administrator or even *your* local police force. Names don't matter but the psychology behind people who occupy these positions of influence is very similar.

So as you read through this book you'll be amused, shocked, angered and uplifted at what you see, and that's just the first chapter! The main point to take away from this book is that you don't have to accept bullying at the hands of court personnel or the police. There are remedies for discriminatory practices most of which will not require that you hire an attorney to pursue. The U.S. government will do it for you. Often times just going one rung up the ladder is enough to set matters straight as well.

I'm giving you the benefit of my experience as a former New Jersey State intern and as the offspring of a now retired New Jersey State employee who taught me the ropes and about cutting through bureaucracy. I am also a New Jersey State Notary Public and a registered law student so while I can not even begin to offer any legal advice, my own personal life experience should offer some insight. I'll be honest. What I don't know, I ask and you should do the same. As an author and internationally syndicated columnist, these are survival skills for my stock in trade. Keeping that last point in mind, I'm truly incredulous that these people would choose to target some-one of my background. Us journalists and authors can crank out a book faster than a sneeze when we're riled enough.

As you walk through these pages take care to note that this is not just another "how to" manual on asserting your rights under our legal system. There is a very human story here as well. You'll see villains wane as heroes emerge. You'll see people who have lost their way in life and in disappointment, lash out to hurt others without reason. There are likewise people in this story who think they are above the very law which they have sworn to uphold.

You'll also see a triumphant spirit who has managed to rise above all of this misery and even see a humorous side to it all. That is the nature of the indomitable human spirit which is mine. To rise above.

Preface

What is in a name? Shakespeare once said, "A rose by any other name would smell just as sweet". How true! All of the names in this book execpt mine are pseudonyms including the town. So don't bother looking up Britville, New Jersey on the map, you won't find it. All the same this could be your town, your county or even your state, so actual names don't matter much here.

If you're wondering about the origin of my surname as it is spelled on the cover with two dots over the "a", it is Hungarian. Its pronounciation from the old country using these accent marks is "Meek-Zock". Now I'm not going to tell you that it was one of the names on the royal court list of the crowned heads of Europe, but I can tell you this. According to a national census done in Hungary in about 1890, the name "Miczak" appears as a family of shopkeepers or small business owners. Humble but hard working people. So I'll leave you with a quote from my most favorite book for both its inspirational and literary value and that is the Bible. It says, "Better than fine oil is a good name."

Speaking of names, I admit I do belong to a somewhat maligned group of professionals called journalists. I write and submit to every major newspaper in N.J. and many of my columns are syndicated in other states across the country and around the world. How we've gotten this bad reputation is by reporting what some would consider "defamatory" statements about public figures, officials and employees. Well, the United States Supreme Court has ruled that many elements of the common law of defamation unduly interfere the the First Amendment guarantees of freedom of speech and the press. Therefore due to the fact that it is more important to leave open those debates concerning those in charge of public affairs, rights of public officials to sue for libel must be limited or free speech will be unduly chilled. *(New York Times v. Sullivan)*

In other words, in order for a public official to sue for libel, he must prove actual malice was present. Actual malice as defined by the U.S. Supreme Court requires that the journalist knew the statement to be false or that he seriously entertained doubts as to the veracity of the statement. In the above cited case of the New York Times v. Sullivan, the burden of proof on the part of the plaintiff was increased. This means that from this case on, the plaintiff must prove actual malice by "clear and convincing evidence" which is higher than the tort "preponderance" standard. That withstanding, you should know that the truth is always a defense to all defamation actions. Statements, articles and even books written in the public interest are also priviledged as they warn readers of acts by individuals capable of injuring the public as a whole. The public official as a plaintiff, would have to *prove* the falsity of the statement as well as the constitutional standard of that degree of fault.

So you see since 1964 the laws concerning defamation have changed drastically and are continuing to do so at a rapid rate. This allows journalists like myself, freedom of the press to report news and chronicle events in the public interest. Having laid this out before you, perhaps you see that I *could* have used the actual names of the public officials and employees who play a part in this story. However, as I mentioned from the outset, names are not important. The acts, on the other hand, are.

Acknowledgements

I'd like to personally thank Chief Albert N. Moskowitz' office of the U. S. Department of Justice in Washington, D.C. as well as the staff and fine detectives of the Monmouth County Prosecutor's Office in helping me to compile the useful information for this book.

List of Abbreviations

ACJC, (Advisory Committee on Judicial Conduct)
DOJ, (Department of Justice, U.S.)

Introduction

My story begins with the local municipal court of sleepy little Britville Borough and has more twists, turns and curves than a hot oiled belly dancer. It is full of lies, deception, favoritism, conspiracy and that's only describing my first day in court! To make a long story short and to spare you all of the gory details, (until later of course), here is an editorial as it appeared in several New Jersey newspapers in the Trenton area:

Dear Editor,

For most, first contact with municipal court comes by way of a traffic ticket. For me, based on a letter written to absentee landlords about a noise problem, I was tried for criminal harassment! Exacting a vendetta, the tenants filed false criminal harassment charges against me for notifying their landlord about them.

This summons was issued without probable cause by Britville's court administrator, Fatima B. Wombat and the trial was with Judge Thuman, (heir to his family's Deli Empire), presiding. It appears that the landlords were friends of Judge Thuman by his own admission from the bench. By the time of my trial, I had written and called the Administrative Office of the Courts several times to complain. Judge Thuman then criticized me for engaging in "a letter writing campaign" for doing so.

After being found "not-guilty", I sued the tenants for malicious prosecution and won 2K. The very next day, the tenant's brother files more false charges against me and I am even arrested without a probable cause hearing! The arrest warrant was signed by Fatima B. Wombat based on the statement of the complainant alone. Since my complaints also were about the court administrator acting under Judge Thuman, this was an act of retaliation working in concert with these disgruntled tenants. This matter has been referred to the Advisory Committee on Judicial Conduct, but I made my first complaint over 9 months ago. Judge Thuman is still active on the bench, exacting retribution just as I predicted he would. I have no prior arrests or conviction for any crime. I am a published author and have been an upstanding, professional member of my community for over 17 years. So don't think this can't happen to you as well!

My next book will chronicle my experiences and what I've learned as a registered law student from this whole ordeal. The working title is *"Inside Justice...Secrets Your Local Court & Police Don't Want You to Know"*, and will be a easy to use guide to accessing agencies, resources and laws designed to protect your rights under both state and federal law. You have the right to be free from unreasonable searches and arrests except by probable cause under the Fourth Amendment. You also have the right to appear before an impartial judge.

Remember, complaining to the local municipal court does no good. If you've had a similar problem and live in New Jersey, contact The Administrative Office of the Courts, Municipal Court Services Division, P.O. Box 989, Trenton, NJ 08625 or call (609) 292-9633. If you live in another state contact your state court administrator.

M.J. Miczak
Britville, NJ

So this was the beginning of this book. The title reflects the fact that much of the information applies to dealing with the court system in most any state. I felt that so much negative energy was going into the constant writing of letters to the Administrative Office of the Courts and the Advisory Committee on Judicial Conduct with really little or no result.

Perhaps the worse consolation of all came from Monmouth County Courthouse who directly oversees both the judge and court administrator, who wrote saying in essence, "Well there's always the appeals process if you get convicted." I don't know about you, but that was a wake up call that I was not dealing with someone interested in protecting my rights, but someone more concerned with maintaining the status quo. In other words, "Don't bother complaining because all of our judges and court people are always right, even when they're wrong."

Going back to the truths upon which the American judicial system was founded, you can look to the Bible. During the Jews departure as free people from Egypt, even Moses accepted help and advice in judging the nation of Israel. His father-in-law in fact told Moses that he would quickly wear himself out trying to decide every case without assistance. So even today the role of a judge has not changed much. A judge must apply the law fairly to all who come before him. If for some reason he feels that he can not with good conscience do so, he has the right or let me correct myself, he has the obligation to recuse himself.

In this way a judge removes from himself any taint of partiality in the case before him. Here is what the Code of Judicial Conduct supports as pertains to the foregoing issue.

Here is the section pertaining specifically to impartiality…

Appendix To Part I
Code of
Judicial Conduct

*[Note: The following Code of Judicial Conduct of the American Bar Association,
as amended by the New Jersey Supreme Court, replaces
the Canons of Judicial Ethics of the American Bar Association.]*

Canon 2. A Judge Should Avoid Impropriety
and the Appearance of Impropriety in All Activities

A. A judge should respect and comply with the law and should act at
all times in a manner that promotes public confidence in the
integrity and impartiality of the judiciary.

B. *A judge should not allow family, social, political, or other relationships to influence judicial conduct or judgment. A judge should not
lend the prestige of office to advance the private interests of others;
nor should a judge convey or permit others to convey the impression
that they are in a special position of influence.* A judge shall not testify as a character witness.

The italicized words show how important recusing oneself can be to the
maintaining of "the integrity of the judiciary". There are many good and
honest judges out there as I have most certainly seen. However isn't it odd
how mostly only the crooked ones make the headline news? Accepting
and soliciting bribes, racial discrimination, sexual improprieties all while
discharging their duties on the bench. The list goes on and on. While you

can not expect to modify or monitor any judge's conduct, you do have the right to appear before an unbiased judge. If you even feel that a judge may not give you a fair shake, you can have your attorney file what is known as an "Affidavit of Prejudice". This is also your right.

Most of us are not even aware that we can complain. There is very little information at the New Jersey Judiciary Website to link you to this information, (**www.judiciary.state.nj.us**).

I'm sure other states have a similar format. As a result, I had to really dig around and call what I thought would be an agency or department to handle this. In contrast, the U.S. Department of Justice's website has extensive information on how and where to file a complaint either civil or criminal under "color of law" provisions which will be discussed in Chapter 5, *Ending the Paper Chase*. They provide clear, direct guidelines as to your rights under these laws and even encourage reprinting of their materials. (see **www.usdoj.gov**) That withstanding the more local state entities may claim that they do not have the same monetary resources as the United States government. This is really just a poor excuse. A simple link button saying, "Complaints", will suffice guys.

Also the process by which New Jersey's Administrative Office of the Court's Municipal Court Services Division handles complaints is risky…to the complainant. Why? Well generally as it done as of this writing, your letter detailing any wrong-doing by court personnel including the judge is sent directly to those parties via the county courthouse. If you have to go back before that same judge, well, let's just say, don't expect a hero's welcome. Many judges find it difficult to take correction. This was the problem in my case. Instead of the judge taking an objective look at what he might not be doing according the Code of Judicial Conduct, he was enraged and did everything possible to retaliate.

Now I'm a Ph.D., a college professor and a registered law student. If a judge did this to me, think about what happens to those who have less education and financial resources to go up against what appears to be a formidable foe. If there is one thing you'll need to understand as you read this book, it is this. Your taxes go to pay that judge and his court employee's salaries. They are employees of the municipal court, and of the city of which they serve, not demigods from outer space.

Keeping this in mind should empower you to move forward and not allow legal garble or the judge's position of authority dissuade or intimidate you. One of the major problems that I've seen has come from dealing with the bureaucrats representing the judiciary. It seems they never tell you anything that will support your position, even though they well know the law and they know that you are in the right. So this is where most people are at a disadvantage. A lay person doesn't have much chance asserting his or her rights if they are not well versed in legalese. Another thing that they do which enrages me is the old diversionary tactic of talking about something else instead of addressing what you just said. Typical scenario:

"But Judge, I was arrested without even having a probable cause hearing!" The bait and switch reply is, "Never mind, you should be aware that you do not have the right to testify at your own probable cause hearing!"

Now what's wrong with this picture? Was I protesting not being able to testify at my own probable cause hearing or was I simply stating *that a probable cause hearing was not held at all?* See what they try to pull? Maybe they think you can't hear or something but I listen to everything that is said to me in court and by the police and you should too. I have an almost uncanny ability to recall exact phases and complete conversations, months even years later. What can I say? I'm a journalist.

As for the other nonsense, I might have believed a lot of what I was told too had I not been in law school and just happened to have a copy of *NJ Court Rules, State & Federal 2000* in my back pocket! However, let's be realistic. The average person just doesn't have access to that kind of information. Often even calling your lawyer who more than likely specializes in real estate or something isn't that helpful either when it comes to needing a quick legal answer.

You may not know this, but most law schools offer their students free access to major legal citation services as part of their tuition. Since almost my first day of class I've had both Lexis and Westlaw on-line services. These citation search engines can be very expensive once you leave law school, (that's why they're free while you're a student just to spoil you), and very few small law firms even use them due to the subscription cost. Oh, but what wonders they can perform! What would take you 3 days to search using casebooks, bound copies of statutes, etc. you can find in 3 minutes on either of these services. You're able to pull up to 20 cases on point at a time to help defend / define your legal issue. There are listings of public records of all sorts to explore as well.

The point here is that change is good but if no one tells Municipal Court Services or any other court supervising agency that something is broken, they are not likely to fix it. In fact, you may find your self being victimized twice. Once by a biased judge and then again for complaining! All the same, do not let that deter you. You have a right and an obligation to yourself to speak up. The state may not want to hear it at first but after awhile, they begin to listen and you may find them to be some of your best allies.

However, if they do not rectify matters within a reasonable amount of time, then move on. I wouldn't give them any more than two months to take action. There are many federal laws which apply to deal with bad judicial conduct, even criminal investigations done by the FBI for some matters. Don't do what I did. I waited and believed that the state of New Jersey would truly handle the matter. Nine months after my initial complaint the same judge was still on the bench, unscathed and bent on revenge for my bringing his deeds to light. Never allow that much time to go by.

I was naive and believed these people. However they were in effect just stringing me along wasting my time and delaying me from filing actions at the federal level. It's like the carrot in front of the donkey. They just keep you going. Meanwhile your situation is worsening, your legal bills mounting, your health deteriorating and no one really cares. Don't fall into this trap. Always remember also that everyone has a boss. What does matter to people is keeping their jobs, so hit em' where it hurts. Contact their supervisor if you're not getting anywhere with them. It's called talking to the next rung up.

This book will show you what to do and not to do using my own experience in writing to various agencies and individuals I've contacted over the past year. Believe me, I have a portfolio full of such letters. I was told by Municipal Court Services, "Keep writing those letters." As a result I have enough to fill a large book which I will now do. Chapter One will introduce you to what happened to me to begin this legal paper chase and how you can deal with your own court problems with suggestions which can fit almost every case in any state. You will learn and benefit from my mistakes and triumphs, hopefully finding a speedy resolution to your own court or police troubles.

Chapter One

The Paper-Chase Begins

I'm relaxing in my home on a Friday afternoon when Sergeant Miller knocks on my door with a summons to appear in court the following Wednesday to answer to charges of criminal harassment. "What?!!!" I'm not sure if I was more shocked or annoyed at this point. I look across the street, there were the tenants of that eyesore of a rental slum, laughing and cheering.

Maintaining my composure I immediately went to my computer, logged into my Westlaw citation service and looked up what I was being charged with. "Let's see, NJSA 2C:33-4,

harassment? For writing a letter to the tenant's landlords about violating the local noise ordinance?" I could find no cases on point that even remotely matched what I did. Not only that, I mailed my letter to the *landlords*, not the tenants. If the tenants got a copy it was because the landlords chose to send it to them. Otherwise how was I harassing them? What is this then, harassment by proxy?

I thought, this must be a mistake by the local court administrator, Fatima B. Wombat. She couldn't have possibly read this letter addressed and sent to these tenant's landlords and surmised that this constituted criminal harassment. I called her up and asked, "Fats, did you actually read my letter?" To this she sharply replied, "Yes, I did!" I'm thinking, is she looking at the same letter? I reply, "No way, Fats!" She didn't even seem to notice that what she typed was not what my letter actually said. My letter complained of yelling and screaming from the tenant's rental property, not the normal use of the premises for sport and recreation.

I then go on to point out that the summons was defective in that it was not served in a timely fashion. The bottom portion clearly stated that you must notify the court of your intention to plead not guilty at least 7 days prior to your court date. I was served on Friday, August 13 th and my arraignment date was that coming Wednesday, August 18th! To this Fats replied, "Oh, just go in and say 'not-guilty' when you go up before the judge!" This was either the sloppiest court administration work I'd ever seen or a railroad job.

Having been served late on a Friday afternoon also put me at a disadvantage because my attorney's office was closed so I didn't get a chance to talk to him until the day before my court appearance. Even without the opportunity of consulting with him, I could see that there was absolutely no probable cause for the issuance of that summons as there is no cause of action for someone complaining about a tenant not adhering to a noise ordinance.

Under the First Amendment we have the right to express our feelings and yes, even to complain, (a field in which I excel especially). Secondly if the summons states "not-guilty" pleas must be lodged 7 days prior to one's court date, it means just that. Municipal court is governed by the same New Jersey Rules of Court which bind every other court in this state. You can't make up the rules as you go along, especially if they unfairly put defendants at a disadvantage by doing so. So what did I learn from this?

Lesson #1

Always read your summons thoroughly. Check also to make sure things like the complainants real name and address are filled in. If not ask why. Also make sure the summons was served in a timely fashion. As noted above if 7 days prior notice is required and the summons is not issued in enough time to provide that, note that also. Lastly have your attorney check the violation you are being charged with. He or she may be able to see if there are any similar cases on the books, (mostly appeals cases). This will show you what rules of law are in play in your case as well.

So I'm thinking to myself concerning this so called court administrator, "This poor misguided soul. I'm sure the judge will catch this major oversight and to make sure he does, I'll send him a certified letter and fax a copy too requesting a dismissal." This I found, turned out to be...

Mistake #1

Never bother writing the judge who is to hear your case. Any criticism of his clerk or court administrator is actually a criticism against him. You see part of the responsibilities of a judge is to supervise his court personnel. If they make mistakes, it embarrasses the judge. However he has the final word and is the one ultimately responsible for what his underlings do. He can be cited with judicial misconduct just for not administering his court room properly. That constitutes an omission in performing his judicial duties.

With that understanding, most of your complaints about court employees should not be written to the judge where they will more than likely end up in the circular file. If you live in New Jersey, you must write or call the Administrative Office of the Courts, Municipal Court Services Division, P.O. 986, Trenton, NJ 08625, (609) 292-9633. They supervise the county courts who have direct supervision over the municipal courts. Your own home state most likely has a similar court supervisory agency who handles such complaints.

Even though my letter to the judge detailed these obvious mistakes, lack of probable cause, untimelyness of the service, etc. Judge Thuman, absolutely ignored it. What incensed me most is that he didn't even bother to read the charges on the face of the summons at my arraignment. I tried to explain that this matter was between me and the landlords, not the tenants. He refused to listen still. Then he imposes court ordered mediation for the tenants and me without the landlords having to attend at all!

This was really preposterous now. "So let me get this straight, these tenants file a false criminal complaint against me based on a letter I wrote and mailed to their landlords, but the landlords to whom the letter was addressed don't have to attend?" I protest and say to Judge Thuman, "Mediation will only work if the landlords are required to attend!" Thuman replies, "This is a matter just between you living people in the neighborhood." I then say, "I want a certificate of disposition or dismissal of this case", to which Judge Thuman replies that this matter isn't going anywhere, (that's right, where could it go in the real world?). He continued that if mediation didn't work he would hear the case.

This was so ridiculous it was surreal. What he was saying is that if mediation didn't work out, I would still be tried for criminal harassment when what I did wasn't a crime? In final exasperation I cry, "But your Honor, this is a baseless complaint!" He then replies in regal tone, "I suggest you not say anything else!" Oh that's right, the court microphones are on and someone might be reviewing this at a later date.

The Mediation Process…My Experience

Mediation even if court ordered is supposed to be voluntary although the court doesn't want to let on that they can't *force* you to participate. Still they really don't need to tie up precious court time with your petty community gripes and grudge matches. The night of this so called mediation just so happened to fall on a night that I had a book signing for my first book. I came early not looking forward to sitting down with this obnoxious couple. Imagine my surprise and horror when they arrive dressed in dirty clothes and the husband absolutely reeking of alcohol! I was so embarrassed that the mediator then knew that we lived in the same neighborhood. I could have crawled under the table right then and there, however a paper bag would have sufficed.

In mediation, the facilitator or mediator is there to help both sides come to an agreement, if possible. Usually this works in minor neighborhood disputes and might have worked if the true objects of my letter of complaint, i.e. the landlords were present.

The mediator is neutral and listens to both sides. Usually the one who filed the complaint goes first. So it went in this session. The female tenant, who we'll call "Hattie" starts in with a rambling dribble of incoherent gossip and juicy tidbits from the neighborhood, none of which has any relevance to the matter at hand. When I was finally given the opportunity to speak, her husband, "Payne" starts pointing his finger in my face screaming that I'd better stop complaining about his family! He was so out of control that the mediator threatened him with removal if he didn't calm down.

I was prepared to settle with a reasonable compromise and quickly as the alcoholic fumes from Payne were displacing all of the available oxygen in the room. Both parties would agree to obey the local noise ordinance. The mediator said, "Well that's just academic because as a matter of law you both *must* obey the local noise ordinance." My point exactly! Well, I guess this was a little too logical for this couple. After all the reason for filing this frivolous complaint in the first place was to retaliate against me for complaining to their landlords, right?

Payne spent the rest of the session being just that, arguing with the mediator who even ended up saying, "You're being unreasonable!" Shortly thereafter they stormed out, refusing to sign even an agreement that both sides would honor the noise ordinance. For the fifth time that night, they threatened that they would file still another criminal complaint against me.

So what's the moral in all of this? Besides not allowing slum lords to move into your neighborhood, never sign a mediation agreement unless you are totally comfortable with its terms. Once signed by both parties, it is a legal contract which can be enforced by the court. If you dishonor or break the mediation agreement, you may find yourself back before the judge explaining why you didn't live up to your side of the agreement.

Most municipalities have a free mediation resolution program. If both parties agree to participate, (see, it's voluntary), then you may be able to work through a few problems before a neutral party. It most certainly beats a gun fight in any case.

Back In Court…My Criminal Trial

Well, the next court date is now my trial. Since Hattie and Payne refused to participate in the mediation program, they get their wish to see me tried before the judge. I felt somewhat likened to a victim of the Spanish Inquisition but I believe those prisoners were shown much more compassion and mercy. The courtroom was completely cleared, all the cases, I mean everything that could have been heard that night was heard. Suddenly the police came in, the doors were shut and the show was on. Right off the bat the judge starts screaming about what a fiasco the mediation was as if this was some great surprise. Since he was looking and yelling at *me* at the time I replied in exasperation, " Your Honor, these people stone-walled that mediation session." Thuman then shouts, "Never mind, the mediation failed for a number of reasons!" Thinking to myself I say, "Oh yeah, that's right and two of those reasons are sitting next to me in court now!"

Things got uglier from there. Thuman then screams, with veins bulging from his neck, (sure sign of an impending stroke), "Miczak, I see that you engaged in a letter writing campaign." Thinking to myself I say, "Wow, is that illegal too? What about breathing, is that o.k.?" Trying to calm him down before having to administer CPR, I calmly reply, "Then I apologize, Your Honor."

"I told you I'd take care of this! I've gotten so many letters back and fourth across my desk because of you!" He wasn't kidding either. By the time I was appearing before him I had written at least two more letters to the Administrative Office of the Courts copying Monmouth County Courthouse. They in turn apparently copied every lawyer and associate on their staff. It was like starting a chain letter. Copy this and mail it to three of your friends.

The trial began with two police officers testifying for the tenants. Amazing how they knew so much about these renters even though they had only lived in the community 2 years and my family has been around for over 17. In any event, an Officer Shoulder gets on the stand first. Now I had just seen him shaking hands and patting Payne on the back in the parking lot on the night of my arraignment so something told me he was going to be a problem. Really, my property taxes go to pay his salary. When didn't he ever shake my hand or pat me on the back?

Shoulder takes the stand and relates how these tenants never make any noise. Humm? I don't remember him owning a house in my neighborhood. Anyway he says that the one day he asked them to turn their music down, it wasn't *really* loud, but he told them if they wanted to be "good guys" to turn it down. Now logic would tell you that if he could hear it in the street, in his police cruiser with the windows rolled up and the air conditioner running, (he never left his vehicle), then it was too loud. Also how can you turn *down* something if the volume wasn't up to begin with?

Next an Officer Total takes the stand. Upon cross examination he really is relating the number of times he came to *my* home as a result of false phone calls by these tenants. I suppose the inference was that I was the only one complaining about these noisy tenants when in fact there are about 20 garden apartments right next door to them who would just as soon not tolerate loud music either. Being closer in proximity to them than I am, they would have even more of a reason to complain.

Next, we'll call him Jed, takes the stand. He and his wife Lacy live in the apartment above Hattie and Payne. He begins complaining that the police are constantly coming to his house every two weeks accusing him of something as if that were my fault too. I'm thinking to myself, "So beating your wife isn't a good enough reason?" Everyone in the neighborhood has seen the police, ambulance and friends rushing to his wife's assistance and Jed being handcuffed and tossed into the back of the patrol car. Still it's always someone else's fault isn't it? Maybe it's his wife's for marrying him.

I finally take the stand in my own behalf, as I had done nothing wrong. As soon as I begin to state how I have lost the peaceful enjoyment of my own property Thuman cuts me off screaming, "So what! My son, (still living at home obviously), works nights and he has to put up with noise!" Oh really? Let's see. You're the local judge for three towns and a practicing lawyer so someone is going to be stupid enough to disturb you or your family? Come on now!

Finally after all of this cat and mouse play, Thuman pronounces me "not-guilty" but threatens if I continue, (continue what, breathing?), perhaps next time I would be found guilty of criminal harassment! That was the absolute last straw. However the real shocker was yet to come. Thuman then says he happens to know the landlords of the tenants and that one of them is even a lawyer. Why is he telling me this? Well, in my letter to his landlord friends, I threatened to sue them if they did not abate the noise problem at their rental property. It appears Judge Thuman was doing them a favor by trying to intimidate me in court and dissuade me from pursuing any legal action against them in the future.

You see any claim or lawsuit, even if it not successful takes time and money to defend. It appeared that I may have had a strong case and the landlords did not want to take the risk of being sued and or losing in civil court. Enter judge friend Thuman.

This sort of nonsense cuts at the very core of confidence in judicial integrity. Often judges such as these are given free reign to dispose of matters, "as they see fit" whether or not by fairly applying the state Rules of Court. In America, many matters are decided by a "gut" feeling whereas in England, the letter of the law is more closely followed. If I had not complained, no one would have ever known about what Judge Thuman had done except him and his landlord acquaintances.

Yes, the Rules of Court do indicate that a court administrator or deputy clerk must accept every complaint, however the JUDGE upon seeing *no probable cause* shall dismiss the case. As they say, "Thems the Rules."

Judges are first and foremost lawyers. Thuman saw there was no probable cause for the court administrator to issue this summons. He saw it, he knew it but refused to dismiss it perhaps in an effort to do his landlord friends a judicial favor.

Lesson # 2

Such things as judicial graft and corruption are not taken lightly by the United States government. Under the U.S. Department of Justice there are many applicable federal laws including the Hobbs Act which are used to investigate similar violations by public officials at the federal, state and local levels. Most violations occur when the official asks, demands, solicits, accepts, receives or agrees to receive something of value in return for influence in the performance of an official act. You can contact your regional Federal Bureau of Investigation office concerning matters of public corruption in the judiciary as well. In New Jersey, you may write or call their New Jersey Field Office:

Federal Bureau of Investigation
1 Gateway Center, 22nd Floor
Newark, NJ 07102-9889
(973) 622-5613

You may read much more about the types of investigations that the FBI does by visiting their very slick website at: **www.fbi.gov**

In the meantime for those of you whom may not yet have Internet access, here is a related section from their FAQ page entitled "Frequently Asked Questions About the FBI":

Does the FBI investigate graft and corruption in local government and in state and local police departments?

Yes. The FBI uses applicable federal laws including the Hobbs Act to investigate violations by public officials in federal, state and local governments. A public official is *any* person elected, appointed, employed or otherwise has a duty to maintain honest and faithful public service. Most violations occur when the official asks, demands, solicits, accepts, receives or agrees to receive something of value in return for influence in the performance of an official act. The categories of public corruption investigated by the FBI include legislative, judicial, regulatory, contractual and law enforcement.

Side Note: As a New Jersey State intern, I worked right down the street from the FBI at the State Building at 1100 Raymond Blvd. My father was a high ranking official in the Department of Transportation and saw to it that I had this opportunity for both my freshman and sophomore years of college.

My most exciting experience as a young intern was attending the opening ceremony of Route 280. There we were arriving in state cars, waiting on the highway span when out of the sky comes a helicopter which lands right on the roadway. Out steps the then Governor Brendan Byrne who greets us, cuts the ribbon and then flies off to his next appointment!

Chapter 2

The Paper Chase Continues

If you think the wheels of justice turn slowly, you haven't seen anything until you file a complaint with your state! As a former state worker I can speak from experience. My father taught me a lot as far as cutting through the red tape. Working for the Department of Transportation for over 30 + years, he learned how to chase down the chain of command. You also have to realize when you complain to the Administrative Office of the Courts, the matter gets referred to either the Advisory Committee on Judicial Conduct if it pertains to a judge or the county courthouse for court personnel.

The real problem is that the way the system is set up now, if you complain, these people are advised of your complaint in detail which may leave you open for retaliation as was in my case. The investigation of the Judge was to be kept confidential by order of the Advisory Committee on Judicial Conduct or the ACJC. However, Judge Thuman was so angered that I had complained about him that he disclosed this matter from the bench in the presence of the press in the courtroom. Not very smart. You see, this is a clear breach in confidentiality of this matter and shows no respect for the proceedings of the ACJC. That in and of itself is a citation of judicial misconduct. However this matter goes much deeper.

This is a case of a judge who sees the victim as the trouble-maker. "If this person didn't complain, I wouldn't be getting investigated", and so fourth. Judges with this sort of attitude are deleterious to the judicial process because they never come to grips with assuming responsibility for their actions. It's always the other guy's fault. This puts the complainant in a very dangerous position because of the long time lapse between your complaint and the outcome of the committee's determinations. During that time, you may well be hauled before the same judge who is harboring a grudge for your complaining against him. This is called a chilling of one's right to protest or complain about judicial misconduct.

The way the system is set up, even if you are in the right, the state gives you very little support leaving most matters up to the discretion of the "judge" you've just complained about. Now that is an example of the fox being left in charge of the quintessential hen house! Expecting a judge to police and monitor himself is really ludicrous. Someone accustomed to being called, "Your honor", is not likely to want to relinquish that distinction. They also may not want to listen to reason when being corrected by their superiors.

However as the Bible says with much eloquence, "Pride goes before a fall." A haughty judge or any one else is not likely to take advice, no matter how good it is. So that pride, leads one to a fall from grace as it were. For a judge that can mean sanctions, disciplinary action up to and including removal from the bench. Since all judges are lawyers, it can also mean being debarred from the state when he or she is licensed. In effect, a ruined reputation and career. Seeing this, you may begin to understand why the many committees monitoring judicial conduct moves slowly to weigh all of the evidence in a complaint against a judge.

This is still no consolation to you as this judge may be maneuvering to make your life miserable as was done in my case. One thing you must understand that such activities by a judge or any other administrator of justice are *illegal*. You are a victim if a judge, based on his relationships or leanings, treats you differently or discriminates against you. You are also a victim if the judge does not appropriately apply the same rules of court to your case as any other.

I had the refreshing opportunity to watch a *real* judge in action when I was doing a story on filing in small claims for a local newspaper. I sat in on the role call with Judge Sultan presiding at Monmouth County Courthouse's Superior Court. He was at the bench on time and called the role of over 145 cases clearly and efficiently in under half an hour.

Cases which were not settled in mediation were heard in his courtroom in a expeditious manner, most being resolved in under fifteen minutes. In that time Judge Sultan took great pains to explain legal concepts clearly to the litigants. He was patient, helpful and quite thorough in his execution of judicial duties. Judge Sultan is also an excellent teacher, somewhat likened to a few of my favorite law professors who have a knack of elucidating murky legal concepts. I think what struck me most about him is his preparation and obvious knowledge and unbiased application of the law.

So I haven't let the poor conduct of one judge jade me entirely. Yet it brings home the point that they are human too, with all the weakness and frailties common the rest of humanity. All the same, since they have accepted this weighty mantle of judging others, they must rise to that standard in both their professional and private lives. If you don't think so, look at the constraints on activities of judges even when they are not on the bench as cited in this section of the Canon on Judicial Conduct:

C. A judge shall not hold membership in any organization that practices invidious discrimination on the basis of race, sex, religion or national origin.

Commentary: Public confidence in the judiciary is eroded by irresponsible or improper conduct by judges. A judge must avoid all impropriety and appearance of impropriety and must expect to be the subject of constant public scrutiny. *A judge must therefore accept restrictions on personal conduct that might be viewed as burdensome by the ordinary citizen and should do so freely and willingly.*

What affiliations a judge may have in her personal life can lead to public scrutiny when she takes the bench. If a judge is concerned that he may be biased in presiding over cases involving friends and relatives, he has the obligation and the privilege to recuse himself. It is as simple as that.

More Letters to
the Administrative Office of the Courts

By now I had already burned out two ink cartridges on my printer writing letters to these people. I wrote them again to detail what happened at my criminal harassment trial which was a mockery in and of itself. Once again my exact letter of complaint was mailed directly to you know who, that's right, Judge Thuman. The Administrative Office of the Courts said that this most recent complaint was sent over to the Advisory Committee on Judicial Conduct for their review. (Oh great, finally then.) All seemed a bit too blasé to me though. Phrases such as "to take any action as they may, (or may not), see fit, etc., etc. abounded in their letters.

Well, three months pass and I gotten no word, Thuman is still on the bench madder than a hornet for me spilling the beans about his doing favors for his landlord friends. I call and leave messages at the Municipal Court Services several times but now my calls are no longer returned. Finally, while responding to a recent thank you letter from my friend, Governor Whitman, I bring the subject up, casually if that's at all possible. Almost immediately I get a letter back from her office that my correspondence had been forwarded to the Advisory Committee on Judicial Conduct . Within a week from that letter, I received my very first letter from the ACJC.

It appears that the governor's letter kick started this review and it wasn't long before the tapes from my criminal trial were shipped down to Trenton, NJ for the committee to listen to. The ACJC asked for any additional information I could provide and I responded by forwarding everything that I had as it related to this case. They kept me updated and apprised of what was going on in this matter from that point on. Wonderful! I was assured that this matter was to be kept confidential until the committee published a decision. I felt confident that my complaint would be in good hands with them. Oh, how wrong I was!

Chapter 3

Getting Even, Legally

My Civil Lawsuit Against the Tenants

As a result of Hattie and Payne's frivolous criminal complaint, I suffered losses of wages and out of pocket expenses as well as lost book sale revenues amounting to over $2,000.00. I felt it would be speedier to resolve the matter in small claims and simply waive the excess. This means that even though your claim comes to over $2,000.00, you are willing to accept the ceiling amount of that particular court which is 2K. I prepared my case with the assistance of my law school chum, Jim Parker, attorneys, citation services and appeared pro se, (that means acting as my own attorney). As I prepared, I wrote the following article to share what I had learned with my readers. See, aren't I generous? Here's the article in its entirety on...

_____

_____

Your Access to the Courts:

Filing A Lawsuit in Small Claims Court

For most of us, our first encounter with the state civil court system may well be in small claims court. As a plaintiff, (person bringing the lawsuit) or defendant, (person being sued), litigants need to know what procedures are associated with the courtroom.

In Monmouth County, people bring their cases to the Small Claims, which is one of the three sections of the Superior Court's Special Civil Part. The other two sections are Landlord/Tenant and regular Special Civil Part. In New Jersey, the limit for the amount you may sue for is $2,000.00. If you believe you are entitled to damages above the ceiling limit of $2,000, you may still sue in Small Claims, but you give up your right to recover damages over $2,000. This is called "waiving the excess" and the additional money can not be claimed later in a separate lawsuit.

What sort of cases can be settled in small claims court? Probably more than you realize. Breach or non-performance on a contract, return of down payments; damage to or loss of property including automobile related accidents, consumer complaints, payment for work performed, bounced checks, and return of rent deposits are only a few of the cases.

Claims that can not be filed include malpractice claims against doctors, dentists or lawyers, alimony or claims arising from a domestic dispute and probate matters, (disputes over a will).

To file a claim, you must go to the Office of the Special Civil Part of the county where at least one of the defendants resides or where his business is located. You must be at least 18 years of age or older, but the lawsuit may be filed by a parent or guardian if under the age of 18. At Monmouth County Courthouse, Court Clerk Caroline Caldwell, Esq. relates, "This whole process may seem a bit intimidating, but there are clerks there in the office to help you. While they can not give you legal advice, they can provide you with procedural information." Here is what you'll need to fill out the form:

- Your full name, address and telephone number. You may fill in the space for your lawyer's telephone number too.

- The correct name(s), address, and telephone number, if available, of each defendant named on the complaint. This is very important for proper service of the lawsuit to the individual, business, etc.
- State the amount of money for which you are suing.
- Say why the defendant owes you money.
- State if there is another case pending between you and the other party and the name of that court.
- State if you will need an interpreter and if so, what language.
- Mention any disabilities which may require special accommodations.
- Sign the completed form.
- Pay the correct filing and service fees at the Central Processing Office and you're done!

Usually service of the lawsuit to the defendant is sent through the regular or certified mail. Service of process is also available by court officer, but you'll need to pay a little extra for his mileage.

Before Sept. 1998, you would have to wait close to a month for the defendant to file an answer to the complaint before getting a trial date. That is now done away with and the defendant now must appear in court to answer at the trial itself. Average time from filing to getting your case on the docket? About one month through Small Claims at Monmouth County Courthouse. Deputy Clerk Donna Yutko recommends coming down to the Special Civil Part office and pick up some informational pamphlcts such as *"Small Claims"* and *"Collecting a Money Judgment".*

Other resources include *"Everybody's Guide to Small Claims Court"* from Nolo Press available on-line at www.nolo.com and Quicken's Family Lawyer 2000 CD-ROM software which offers a small claims worksheet to organize your case. You may also visit the New Jersey Judiciary Homepage at: **www.judiciary.state.nj.us**

Well, I tell you all of this research paid off. I won 2K hands down! To get someone on malicious prosecution you must prove all four elements as follows:

1.) **That the person instituted criminal or quasi criminal proceedings against you**
2.) **That there was *no probable cause* for the complaint**
3.) **That the ruling ended in your favor**
4.) **That there was Malice on the part of the filer**

During the proceeding I brought in evidence that Hattie had feigned probable cause by lying and saying that I had mailed her the infamous "landlord letter" to make it appear as if I were harassing her via direct mail or something. The smoking gun came in the form of a letter sent from the landlord to my lawyer admitting that he himself forwarded the letter to Hattie and Payne along with a Notice to Cease, (the noise), and a copy of the local noise ordinance.

SIDE BAR
Probable Cause…Why it's Needed Before
a Summons or Arrest Warrant is Issued

Let's pause for a "side-bar" here in case you're not sure about how important probable cause is before deputy clerks or court administrators write up a summons for someone to appear in court:

"The matter is somewhat different in the case of a summons (as opposed to an arrest warrant), because of its qualitatively different consequences vis-à-vis deprivation of freedom. A summons in lieu of a warrant is not however without consequence since it initiates the criminal process, compels appearance to answer the complaint and may lead to the routine issuance of an arrest warrant upon the failure of appearance. For that determination to be made by the complaining

witness and for the summons to issued over his signature is fundamentally offensive." 189 N.J. Super. 67, 74, 458 A. 2d 1299, 1302-1303

In other words probable cause must be present before a summons can be issued by the court administrator, deputy clerk or court clerk. Probable cause is absolutely required before an arrest or search warrant is issued by the *Judge*. Remember this last point because we'll come back to it in Chapter 4, *An Arresting Development.*

Something else was disclosed during my lawsuit against Hattie. She said that when she went to try to get transcripts from my criminal trial they had been sent to Trenton because I had complained about Judge Thuman. Wait a minute. Didn't the Advisory Committee on Judicial Conduct tell me this matter was to be kept totally confidential pending the conclusion of their investigation? How did Hattie know then? Well, the person she would have to ask to access those court transcripts was none other than Fatima B. Wombat, the Britville court administrator who wouldn't be able to recognize probable cause if it kicked her. Likewise how would Fatima B. Wombat know that I had complained about the judge, aka, her boss? That's right, Judge Thuman. Oh brother. Small town, big mouths.

Upon the Judge Sultan handing down the judgment in my favor, Hattie and Payne ran out of the courtroom without making any arrangements for payment. Some nerve.

Lesson #3

Do not assume that just because you've won a judgment that you will automatically be paid. Truth is most judicial judgments go uncollected. You have to know if your adversary has assets and if so where they might be. There are some agencies which will collect judicial judgments, but many of them want up to 50% of the purse. A little too greedy for me guys.

As of this writing if is still fair game to hire an investigator to locate your deadbeat's assets, nonetheless a bill recently signed by President Bill Clinton under the Privacy Act, may make this a bit more difficult in the future. If you have a bonefide judicial judgment, most likely your right to search for the defendant's "chattels", (I just love that word, don't you?), will remain intact. The act is really designed to limit your neighbor from peeking into your finances just for laughs or gloating privileges upon finding you have less money than he does.

Perhaps the best thing to do is to file a bank levy…immediately. If you have the person's real name and not some fictitious alias as was the case with "Hattie", you can post a bank levy on that account if it has his or her name on it. How does that happen? You fill out a simple form with where your adversary has a bank account, (you don't need an account number). The court officer then goes to the bank and presents the levy, sort of like a legal "bank hold-up".

The result? Your opponents assets are frozen like custard. They can put money in but they can't take it out. Any checks written on that account will then bounce like rubber. You then file a motion to turn over funds and if the person doesn't come up with a good reason why you shouldn't have the money, viola', it is yours. Remember, you only get up to the total amount of your judgment in the account at the time. So if there's only $200.00, you apply this against the balance of your total judgment. You can file more bank levies to get the rest of your money, but I think by the first time around, your opponent will have sense enough to move their funds elsewhere. Then again, you never know.

Also when the court officer comes to the bank, he adds his *own* charges to the judgment for coming out there, (hey, this man deserves a fair wage for his work). Believe me, these people work hard and are not amused with deadbeats using phony names or aliases. This wastes both your time and theirs in trying to collect a judgment you've been rightfully awarded.

If this happens, that is if you find the person has been using an alias, simply return to the court and file a motion to amend the name of the defendant to their real name. This way, you'll be able to collect under both names and there is no charge for filing this additional motion. The court officer then goes before the judge and if the judge grants the motion, back to the bank he goes for your money. See lying doesn't pay after all, does it?

Speaking of lying, this is the perfect sagway into Chapter 4 where you will not believe what happens next!

Chapter 4

An Arresting Development

Winning money in my case against Hattie for malicious prosecution in court that day wasn't the only reason why I took her to court. It was more of a matter of principal. I was obviously not starving with or without the 2K so there was something deeper at stake. That was my reputation. I did not do what she said I did. It is not harassment of the tenants to complain to a landlord about their not obeying the same local ordinances we are all bound by. I pay hefty taxes on my home. In contrast, these people rent. Still they have the privilege to live in a nice neighborhood, but they don't appreciate it. Instead of trying to fit in, they stand out like sore thumbs because they are so inconsiderate.

Getting Hattie before an impartial judge was so very refreshing because he applied the rules of law as they should have been from the start. Judge Sultan, who presided over my civil case even said, "Well you can clearly see on the face of this summons that there was no probable cause for its issuance. Someone calling you up on the phone at 3 am in the morning is harassment. A letter to your landlord like this is not. In fact, I am really surprised that the court administrator even signed this, (remember Fatima B. Wombat?). *She shouldn't have signed it.*"

Vindication in full! This is what I told the state, this is what I told the county, this is what I told Judge Thuman and this is what I told Pat Wombat. **NO PROBABLE CAUSE**. Was I speaking a different language or something? Of course not. These people all know the rules of law which govern our courts. For one reason or another, perhaps fearing lawsuits, they were reluctant to stand up for me and say, "You know, this is wrong." By trying to make me think that I had done something wrong when I really didn't is perhaps the most sinister of the acts perpetrated upon me by Judge Thuman. He used his judicial cloak to masquerade as a representative of justice.

So here the matter was settled much to my satisfaction by an unbiased judge. Everyone present took note of an injustice delivered at the hands of the court administrator and supported by the presiding municipal court judge.

Lesson #4

What I've learned up to this point is not to allow yourself to be brainwashed. Look at what you are being charged with. Do you see anyone else in jail for doing the same thing? How many people each year in New York write letters to absentee landlords about over crowding, run down appearance of the property, noise, drug dealing, prostitution, etc. These all constitute "maintaining or continuing a private nuisance" and you don't have to put up with it.

In New Jersey in order to win such a case the activity must be both "unlawful and unreasonable" to be defined as a nuisance. Other states which have a similar definition are Kentucky, New Mexico, North and South Dakota, Oklahoma. Other states do not have such a stipulation, so you'll need to check.

Also, for such encroachments on your enjoyment and usefulness of your property you can sue the landlord and/or neighbors over and over again should they continue. Why? Well, all you are able to get are compensatory damages or those damages recoverable for the precise injury sustained. These may include compensation for your loss of sleep or your inability to carry on normal activity without interference. In this matter the court can not order an injunction in the matter demand that they stop. They just don't have that kind of authority in such a case. Usually being taken to court for a few hundred dollars each time is enough to quiet them down though. Keep in mind that if this is going on in your neighborhood, then you my friend, are the victim, not the tenants who are whining that you're picking on them.

The First Amendment guarantees your right to freedom of speech. That includes peaceful forms of protest such as "engaging in a letter writing campaign" if you're so inclined. You see, some people for their own selfish purposes would like to criminalize every activity that annoys them personally, even one which includes telling the truth. Fortunately, that's not what our Constitution is based on, that is the subjective test which some would like to employ. "I don't like what you're saying or writing so you should go to jail", is as draconian as burning people at the stake for reading. So it goes for those who would twist the law to make criminals out of those whom they disagree with.

This is why the wisdom of the law shines if it is not buried. Look here at the following citation from New Jersey's books:

"The criminal and quasi-criminal system is neither designed nor intended to provide a vehicle for the raising and settlement of purely private disputes." 189 N.J. Super. 67, 74, 458 A. 2d 1299, 1303

This follows just what I have stated supra or above. Our criminal courts are not designed for the purpose of handling neighborhood grudge matches and petty cat fights. Go to civil court for those!

In my case, I had no idea that the judge was biased against me until the end of my criminal trial. Now that I know, however, I will have my attorney's file what is known as an "Affidavit of Prejudice" if this judge isn't removed from the bench, (let's all write letters, shall we?), or takes an extended lifetime vacation to Nome, Alaska.

An Affidavit of Prejudice does not need to show the whys or wherefores of your desire not to appear before a certain judge. Perhaps you don't like the way he parts his hair and based on that, you feel he won't give you a fair shake because you part yours on the other side. Good enough! You have the right to file that motion. The better solution is to get bad judges off the bench in the first place, but we can only hope.

More Lies, More False Complaints, and Now an Arrest

Its early spring, everyone is outside cleaning up, airing out and freshening up. This is just one day after I won my judgment against Hattie. Even with my win, I was uneasy. She had vowed to file another false criminal complaint against me and was set on retaliation if it killed her.

What struck me most is through out the proceedings, the woman showed no remorse for lying. She even had the guts to file a phony counter claim suing *me* for $2,000.00 for bugging her. How was I doing that? By keeping my house in good repair and by being quiet? Hattie was even more crocked than I had imagined! Even so there was something very sinister in her eyes, a dark, evil hatred that I can not to this day begin to comprehend.

Remember that Hattie hadn't lived in the neighborhood long. Actually my family was the first only homeowners on the street to go over and welcome her into the neighborhood with food, toys and clothes for both her and her children, all of which she gladly accepted. Jealousy, envy, watching too many soap operas, who knows what turned her. The point was that she had made a career out of spreading lies about me and my family. "Stay away from them, they're bad people!" she would scream to the children of people who just moved in. I'm thinking, I've been here for 17 years and I know all of my neighbors by name. Why was she so set on turning people away from us? One may never know, but in any event, I have a very rich life outside of Britville with all of the colleges, historical societies and charities I belong to and true friends at my house of worship. Amen.

In any event, that day, something told me to call the county prosecutor's office and report this case for a perjury indictment. Something needed to be done. It's just not right that she should lie and get others into trouble. Who would be next then? Someone who has a nicer car than hers? A woman who is prettier? Where does it stop? Just lie on someone and get them sent to jail? Is that how it works? This is deranged.

I really did not get a true picture of what I was dealing with until I contacted the Monmouth County Prosecutor's office and spoke with Deputy Chief Menorah. Menorah was very astute in summing up the situation quickly. I told him that I had just taken Hattie to court and won a judgment for malicious prosecution but she has vowed to file another false complaint. Menorah was sharp and suggested immediately that I talk to my attorney about getting a civil restraining order against her. He then told me that this case intrigued him and that he would have one of his detectives contact me either that afternoon or Monday. As it turned out Detective Dryer called me that afternoon. "I know she's going to try something", I told him. Dryer was very reassuring and considerate. He took the time to discuss what could be done and we made an appointment to meet the following Wednesday so that he could take my statement.

I had only just hung up the phone when less than an hour latter, two police officers appear on my front porch. Thinking they were there due to an emergency in the neighborhood, I asked if they wanted to come in. They said no, and asked if I would step outside. I'm thinking there is something they need me to see or something. Not even close! When I step out onto my porch, the officer says he has a warrant for my arrest. I ask what am I being arrested for? He says stalking! This was so preposterous!

Once again, dancing on her front porch across the street was Hattie, almost going into convulsions with laughter. I'm thinking, "This woman needs to be put away, and lose the key while you're at it!" So I'm read my Miranda warnings, I'm hand-cuffed, and put into the back of the police car and taken to Britville Police Station. There I was placed in a cell. Back home my front door was left unlocked with my two children left upstairs not knowing what had happened to me. My oldest child quickly summed up the situation seeing Hattie dancing in the middle of the street singing, "Somebody got arrested!". I called them from the police station. They were beyond consolation.

While I was there, the police wanted to question me. I refused to answer any questions until my lawyer arrived. My attorney, Rich Poser,

Esq. is in New York so they knew they had a long wait! Sergeant Joe Miller then calls…yes, him again, Judge Thuman who says "ROR, (released on own recognizance) in lieu of $1,000.00 bail ."

When I'm finally allowed to look at the arrest warrant, (I wasn't at my door), I wanted to laugh but I was too annoyed. Once again this ninny of a court administrator, Fats Wombat signs both a summons and arrest warrant for the same alleged offense for the same day. Not only that, *she issues the arrest warrant* based solely on the statement of the complainant!

Even more outrageous is the fact that she didn't even go before a judge to get the arrest warrant signed. She signs it herself. And just who was this complainant accusing me of stalking him and company? None other than Hattie's brother! You see, it would look too obvious if Hattie signed another phony complaint, as she had promised to do. So she gets big brother to do it instead. Obviously perjury runs in the family. No probable cause hearing was done whatsoever, either. This screams litigation. I have never been arrested in my life, now because of these liars I have an arrest record? I'm fingerprinted but not photographed for mug shots because the Britville police just couldn't find any more film for the camera. Bummer and I just had my hair cut at the barber's for the occasion. Well, my family came for my release and were they ever mad. They had every reason to be.

As soon as I got home, even though it was the weekend, I began calling, faxing and screaming at all of these bureaucrats whom I had been writing and calling over the past nine months. In all this time, a whole new human being could have been brought into this world. At least that would have been more than they accomplished.

I called everyone on my list and then some including my lawyers and the press. By the time Monday rolled around I was on the phone again. Someone from the ACJC mustered the courage and returned my call. Poor man who was in no way involved in this melee, had to listen to screams of "I got arrested you fool!"

Now I had to be arraigned before, guess who…that's right, Judge Thuman. I wanted to tell him we had to stop meeting like this, but I didn't want to hurt his feelings. This time I was a bit better prepared because I brought the press with me. Works better than a lawyer, exposing courtroom corruption to the light of day, but what happened next totally floored even me.

In the presence of the press and in front of the whole Britville Borough police department, assembled just to see me shot down in flames I guess, Judge Thuman did the unthinkable. He breached the confidentiality of the ACJC's investigation of his performance on the bench! Gasp! A hush fell over the courtroom. In his anger against me, he betrayed a judicial confidence by blabbing that I had filed a complaint against him with the ACJC. I don't know how you can get any more unprofessional than that, but there you have it.

More of the same bogus charges as usual, but at this point I am thoroughly disgusted. After Thuman takes all that time reading me the Riot Act, he doesn't even ask how I am pleading. So I say, "I'm pleading not-guilty!" and blew out of his courtroom. It is really perturbing that my tax dollars are going to support this foolishness. Yours too for that matter. This is what's called assuring job security for municipal court workers well into retirement. File all sorts of ridiculous complaints and lock up the court schedule for less important issues such as drunk driving convictions and assault cases.

Chapter 5

Ending the Paper Chase

It seems that things finally began to come together when I contacted the county prosecutor's office. I had been writing the Administrative Office of the Courts for 9 months. I had been writing the ACJC now since February and matters only had gotten worse. I was so jaded by the lack of action which was being taken against this judge, I didn't have much faith in the Prosecutor's Office either. I was wrong. Contacting them was the best thing I had done thus far in this case. Why? Well, get a clue, (pardon the pun), they are DETECTIVES. They are trained to listen, observe and remember details. They are able to quickly discern discrepancies. They also have a higher knowledge of criminal law than most in law enforcement. When I came in and finally met Detective Dryer, he was everything I would imagine a detective would be but with one added dimension. Compassion.

You can tell a lot about a person by the way they shake your hand. There was a lot of character in Dryer's handshake. Firm, assured, steady. Having watched a few too many episodes of *Law and Order*, I was expecting a gloomy, dismal interrogation room. Not even close. All of the offices were clean and modern with detectives coming in and out dressed more like Wall Street professionals. They even smiled.

I gave my statement to Detectives Wendell and Dryer which was being typed as I spoke by the typist with a wise-cracking sense of humor honed from working within that department for many years. Immediately Wendell and Dryer began to pick things up, piece by piece, item by item. Things that I had missed even after looking at the same documents for months they spotted immediately. Man, these guys were good!

I even showed them Hattie's brother's new set of false criminal complaints. They immediately saw problems with those documents as well. I told the detectives that I believe this was the same guy who harassed and assaulted me back in August of last year. I called the police when it happened and wanted to press charges but didn't know who he was or his name. Everytime I asked Britville P.D. for incident reports, I got a different story everytime such as:

"Have your lawyer subpoena them. What do you need them for? We don't have to generate incendent reports unless you pressed charges at the time, etc." Excuses, excuses. Finally I just ended up hiring my own detective. For more information on how to obtain incident reports or other police records from you local police department skip to Chapter 6. Cited there is an example of the NJ law on the books, but it will also show you who you might contact in your own state.

Lesson #5

What I gained most from meeting with Detectives Wendell and Dryer is that at some point in time, you are going to have to abandon the paper chase. Letter writing to the degree that I have been asked to do is time consuming and to a point futile. It takes you away from more proactive options such as what I have just described and those which I will later show in this same chapter.

Perjury is a crime. This was the first question I asked of Municipal Court Services. "This woman has obviously lied to file this complaint, so why isn't she being prosecuted for perjury?" I never got an answer to that question from them. If a judge knows that someone has committed perjury, that is lied under oath, then he is under obligation as both an attorney and judge to report it.

Also it is often the prosecutor's office or in New York, the "D.A." who will most often handles cases of police misconduct. If you have a minor issue, let's say an officer is nasty or unprofessional, you can report it to the chief of police in your local municipality. Such matters are easily handled internally without having to be referred out to the county level.

Matters of a litigious nature such as perjury, sexual misconduct, etc. have to be referred out and addressed by the prosecutor's office. They will do a thorough investigation into the matter and even prosecute if there is enough evidence of wrong doing.

Additionally if you have experienced long standing or repeated acts of discrimination, there are other remedies available as discussed at the U.S. Department of Justice's website at: **www.usdoj.gov**

If you look under the Civil Rights Division, you'll see many federal laws which apply under what are broadly known as 42 USC and 18 USC. These are federal laws that make it a crime for one or more persons acting under *color of law* to willfully deprive or conspire to deprive another person of any right protected by the Constitution or laws of the United States.

Here is a printout from their website on the laws and remedies available to deal with such problems:

U.S. Department of Justice
Civil Rights Division

ADDRESSING POLICE MISCONDUCT

LAWS ENFORCED BY THE
UNITED STATES DEPARTMENT OF JUSTICE

The vast majority of the law enforcement officers in this country perform their very difficult jobs with respect for their communities and in compliance with the law. Even so, there are incidents in which this is not the case. This document outlines the laws enforced by the United States

Department of Justice (DOJ) that address police misconduct and explains how you can file a complaint with DOJ if you believe that your rights have been violated.

Federal laws that address police misconduct include both criminal and civil statutes. These laws cover the actions of State, county, and local officers, including those who work in prisons and jails. In addition, several laws also apply to Federal law enforcement officers. The laws protect all persons in the United States (citizens and non-citizens).

Each law DOJ enforces is briefly discussed below. In DOJ investigations, whether criminal or civil, the person whose rights have been reportedly violated is referred to as a victim and often is an important witness. DOJ generally will inform the victim of the results of the investigation, but we do not act as the victim's lawyer and cannot give legal advice as a private attorney could.

The various offices within DOJ that are responsible for enforcing the laws discussed in this document coordinate their investigation and enforcement efforts where appropriate. For example, a complaint received by one office may be referred to another if necessary to address the allegations. In addition, more than one office may investigate the same complaint if the allegations raise issues covered by more than one statute.

What is the difference between criminal and civil cases?

Criminal and civil laws are different. Criminal cases usually are investigated and handled separately from civil cases, even if they concern the same incident. In a criminal case, DOJ brings a case against the accused person; in a civil case, DOJ brings the case (either through litigation or an administrative investigation) against a governmental authority or law enforcement agency. In a criminal case, the evidence must establish proof "beyond a reasonable doubt," while in civil cases the proof need only satisfy the lower standard of a "preponderance of the evidence." Finally, in criminal cases, DOJ seeks to punish a wrongdoer for past misconduct through imprisonment or other sanction. In civil cases, DOJ seeks to correct a law enforcement agency's policies and practices that fostered the misconduct and, where appropriate, may require individual relief for the victim(s).

Federal Criminal Enforcement

It is a crime for one or more persons acting under color of law willfully to deprive or conspire to deprive another person of any right protected by the Constitution or laws of the United States. (18 U.S.C. §§ 241, 242). "Color of law" simply means that the person doing the act is using power given to him or her by a governmental agency (local, State, or Federal). A law enforcement officer acts "under color of law" even if he or she is exceeding his or her rightful power. The types of law enforcement misconduct covered by these laws include excessive force, sexual assault, intentional false arrests, or the intentional fabrication of evidence resulting in a loss of liberty to another. Enforcement of these provisions does *not* require that any racial, religious, or other discriminatory motive existed.

What remedies are available under these laws?

Violations of these laws are punishable by fine and/or imprisonment. There is no private right of action under these statutes; in other words, these are not the legal provisions under which you would file a lawsuit on your own.

Federal Civil Enforcement

"Police Misconduct Provision"

This law makes it unlawful for State or local law enforcement officers to engage in a pattern or practice of conduct that deprives persons of rights protected by the Constitution or laws of the United States. (42 U.S.C. § 14141). The types of conduct covered by this law can include, among other things, excessive force, discriminatory harassment, false arrests, coercive sexual conduct, and unlawful stops, searches or arrests. In order to be covered by this law, the misconduct must constitute a "pattern or practice"—it may not simply be an isolated incident. The DOJ must be able to show in court that the agency has an unlawful policy or that the incidents constituted a pattern of unlawful conduct. However, unlike the other civil laws discussed below, DOJ does not have to show that discrimination has occurred in order to prove a pattern or practice of misconduct.

What remedies are available under this law?

The remedies available under this law do not provide for individual monetary relief for the victims of the misconduct. Rather, they provide for injunctive relief, such as orders to end the misconduct and changes in the agency's policies and procedures that resulted in or allowed the misconduct. There is no private right of action under this law; only DOJ may file suit for violations of the Police Misconduct Provision.

Title VI of the Civil Rights Act of 1964 and the "OJP Program Statute"

Together, these laws prohibit discrimination on the basis of race, color, national origin, sex, and religion by State and local law enforcement agencies that receive financial assistance from the Department of Justice.

(42 U.S.C. § 2000d, *et seq.* and 42 U.S.C. § 3789d(c)). Currently, most persons are served by a law enforcement agency that receives DOJ funds. These laws prohibit both individual instances and patterns or practices of discriminatory misconduct, *i.e.,* treating a person differently because of race, color, national origin, sex, or religion. The misconduct covered by Title VI and the OJP (Office of Justice Programs) Program Statute includes, for example, harassment or use of racial slurs, unjustified arrests, discriminatory traffic stops, coercive sexual conduct, retaliation for filing a complaint with DOJ or participating in the investigation, use of excessive force, or refusal by the agency to respond to complaints alleging discriminatory treatment by its officers.

What remedies are available under these laws?

DOJ may seek changes in the policies and procedures of the agency to remedy violations of these laws and, if appropriate, also seek individual remedial relief for the victim(s). Individuals also have a private right of action under Title VI and under the OJP Program Statute; in other words, you may file a lawsuit yourself under these laws. However, you must first exhaust your administrative remedies by filing a complaint with DOJ if you wish to file in Federal Court under the OJP Program Statute.

Title II of the Americans with Disabilities Act of 1990 and Section 504 of the Rehabilitation Act of 1973

The Americans with Disabilities Act (ADA) and Section 504 prohibit discrimination against individuals with disabilities on the basis of disability. (42 U.S.C. § 12131, *et seq.* and 29 U.S.C. § 794). These laws protect all people with disabilities in the United States. An individual is considered to have a "disability" if he or she has a physical or mental impairment that substantially limits one or more major life activities, has a record of such an impairment, or is regarded as having such an impairment.

The ADA prohibits discrimination on the basis of disability in all State and local government programs, services, and activities regardless of whether they receive DOJ financial assistance; it also protects people who are discriminated against because of their association with a person with a disability. Section 504 prohibits discrimination by State and local law enforcement agencies that receive financial assistance from DOJ. Section 504 also prohibits discrimination in programs and activities conducted by Federal agencies, including law enforcement agencies.

These laws prohibit discriminatory treatment, including misconduct, on the basis of disability in virtually all law enforcement services and activities. These activities include, among others, interrogating witnesses, providing emergency services, enforcing laws, addressing citizen complaints, and arresting, booking, and holding suspects. These laws also prohibit retaliation for filing a complaint with DOJ or participating in the investigation.

What remedies are available under these laws?

If appropriate, DOJ may seek individual relief for the victim(s), in addition to changes in the policies and procedures of the law enforcement agency. Individuals have a private right of action under both the ADA and Section 504; you may file a private lawsuit for violations of these statutes. There is no requirement that you exhaust your administrative remedies by filing a complaint with DOJ first.

How to File a Complaint with DOJ

Criminal Enforcement

If you would like to file a complaint alleging a violation of the criminal laws discussed above, you may contact the Federal Bureau of Investigation (FBI), which is responsible for investigating allegations of criminal deprivations of civil rights. You may also contact the United States Attorney's Office (USAO) in your district. The FBI and USAOs have offices in most major cities and have publicly-listed phone numbers. In addition, you may send a written complaint to:

Criminal Section
Civil Rights Division
U.S. Department of Justice
P.O. Box 66018
Washington, D.C. 20035-6018

Civil Enforcement

If you would like to file a complaint alleging violations of the Police Misconduct Statute, Title VI, or the OJP Program Statute, you may send a written complaint to:

Coordination and Review Section
Civil Rights Division
U.S. Department of Justice
P.O. Box 66560
Washington, D.C. 20035-6560

You may also call the Coordination and Review Section's toll-free number for information and a complaint form, at (888) 848-5306 (voice and TDD).

If you would like to file a complaint alleging discrimination on the basis of disability, you may send a written complaint to:

> Disability Rights Section
> Civil Rights Division
> U.S. Department of Justice
> P.O. Box 66738
> Washington, D.C. 20035-6738

You may also call the Disability Rights Section's toll-free ADA Information Line at (800) 514-0301 (voice) or (800) 514-0383 (TDD).

How do I file a complaint about the conduct of a law enforcement officer from a Federal agency?

If you believe that you are a victim of criminal misconduct by a Federal law enforcement officer (such as the Immigration and Naturalization Service; the FBI; the Customs Service; Alcohol, Tobacco, and Firearms; or the Boarder Patrol), you should follow the procedures discussed above concerning how to file a complaint alleging violations of the criminal laws we enforce. If you believe that you have been subjected by a Federal law enforcement officer to the type of misconduct discussed above concerning "Federal Civil Enforcement," you may send a complaint to the Coordination and Review Section, at the address listed above. That office will forward your complaint to the appropriate agency and office.

What information should I include in a complaint to DOJ?

Your complaint, whether alleging violations of criminal or civil laws listed in this document, should include the following information:

Your name, address, and telephone number(s). The name(s) of the law enforcement agency (or agencies) involved. A description of the conduct you believe violates one of the laws discussed above, with as many details as possible. You should include: the dates and times of incident(s); any injuries sustained; the name(s), or other identifying information, of the officer(s) involved (if possible); and any other examples of similar misconduct. The names and telephone numbers of witnesses who can support your allegations. If you believe that the misconduct is based on your race, color, national origin, sex, religion, or disability, please identify the basis and explain what led you to believe that you were treated in a discriminatory manner (i.e., differently from persons of another race, sex, etc.).

Reproduction of this document is encouraged.
www.usdoj.gov/crt/split/documents/polmis.htm
Last updated October 13, 1999

Chapter 6

Secrets Your Locals Don't Want You to Know

With the information you now have at your disposal from Chapter 5, perhaps you'll see that such powerful laws are something your local police or court administrator doesn't want you to know about. I mean, how often do you hear, "Oh don't bother me with this. Go take it up with the Federal Government!" from your town's chief of police? That's right, its unheard of. This is because taking your complaint out of the locality may provide you with access to investigators who will apply the letter of the law to your case and be less partial.

You see, in each state there is a chain of command but they are all yet one family. Just like a parent not liking to hear a bad report about their child's conduct, so it often goes at the county and municipal level as well. Also fear of litigation, that is lawsuits and the bad publicity that sort of thing brings in its wake are not desirable commodities to them. This is why I advise you to end the paper chase as soon as possible. If you haven't gotten anywhere in 2 months, trust me you won't in 9 either. Also, many of the federal filings in Chapter 5 require that you report the incident within 180 days of its occurrence. If you let the local entities tie up your time by telling you, "We're looking into it", you may be missing that window of opportunity to have your case filed and prosecuted.

Another fact akin to the parent-child analogy is the fact that locally, most everyone knows each other. The local judge may play golf with the county prosecutor, or they may attend other events on a regular basis. Quite frankly they're workmates. When you complain about one, you may appear the villain because you are speaking ill of someone whom they've developed a working relationship with over the years. Those ties are strong and true so don't underestimate them when you file a complaint locally. You need to get your case heard by an agency who is not going to be influenced by such relationships. Now unless your local county prosecutor plays golf with Janet Reno every third Wednesday, you should be all right in filing a federal complaint.

A similar thing happened to my father when he was employed by the State of New Jersey. His immediate supervisor was very oppressive and even a bit jealous of my father's ability to study and pass the many civil service exams needed to advance to higher levels of authority in the Department of Transportation. Truly showing his tenacity, he was not one to back down however. This brought him into continuous confrontations with his supervisor.

My father quickly learned to skip over the "middle man" and take his beef directly to the state commissioner whom I can only remember as being a Mr. Pitmann in Trenton. I can remember meeting him on the many trips my father took me on to visit the state capital. Pitmann respected my father for his contributions to the department and appreciated his intelligence and knack for organization. Often, he decided issues fairly in my father's favor and after a while his boss didn't bother trying to ride him any longer. It just wasn't worth the trouble!

My father, in contrast to his boss, was well suited for management of those employed under him. He was strict, by the book, (being a former Marine Sergeant), but very fair and his men respected him for that when they came to him with their disputes. I can remember around the holidays his men giving him gifts of fruit cakes, Polish dumplings, home canned cherries and the like. Before my father was ready to retire in his late 50's, he had passed the state exams to become a supervisor at the state office in Trenton. He had made it! However, he decided to take an early retirement instead since he had put his time in and to this day collects a healthy pension. There's a saying about working for the state. You don't make much while you're working, but do they ever take care of you after you retire. I've surely seen this to be the case.

The point that I'm trying to make is that once again, local prejudices and jealousies are common. It's human nature. Take your complaint to a less biased arena where the office really doesn't know either of you and you'll have a greater chance at an equitable solution.

Mistake #3

You have the right in most states to access police reports. They are a matter of public record which you pay taxes to have on file and obtain. Never assume that the local police are going to let you know this. In New Jersey, the rules which govern this are under Executive Order Number 69. It deals with records of local police departments and your ability to get copies. Part 3, section a. states:

"Where a crime has been reported but no arrest yet made, information as to the type of crime, time location and type of weapon if any;"

This would commonly be known as an incident report. Also, you might not know that you can still file charges up to one year after the incident occurred. So this is why incident reports are as a matter of procedure required to be kept by local police stations. Often times you'll see people in court with such reports obtained from the officer or station who responded to the call at the time.

Whether or not you chose at that point to press charges at the time of the crime or not is immaterial to the generation of the police department's reporting of the incident. When you decide to press charges, that is another document called a *summons* which will call that person into court to answer for the alleged crime. Two separate actions, two separate documents. So if your local police station hems and haws about providing them or starts asking you what do you need them for or other such nonsense, what are you going to say?

That's right, "I'll just put in a request through the prosecutor's office" and leave.

Section J. of Executive Order 69 states that the county prosecutor shall promptly resolve all disputes as to whether or not the release of records would be otherwise be inappropriate between the records custodian and any person seeking access to them. So the bottom line is that the final word as to whether or not you can have copies of incident reports rests with the prosecutor's office, not the local police precinct.

Once again your state most likely has a similar provision on the books. You can see New Jersey State's document on-line by visiting: **www.state.nj/lps/dcj/agguide/exec69.htm** or take a look at it in its entirety as provided here:

RECORDS OF POLICE DEPARTMENTS

Executive Order No. 69
Issued May 1997(3/98)

RECORDS OF POLICE DEPARTMENTS

WHEREAS, Chapter 73, P.L. 1963, as amended, finds and declares it to be the public policy of this State that public records shall be readily accessible for examination by the citizens of this State for the protection of the public interest except as otherwise provided in said law; and

WHEREAS, some limitation upon the right to examine and copy records provided by Chapter 73 is essential and not detrimental to the public interest as recognized by existing statutory and common law; and

WHEREAS, disclosure of information must be consistent with existing statutory law regarding confidentiality in certain areas; and

WHEREAS, said Chapter 73 provides that records which would otherwise be deemed to be public records, subject to inspection and examination and available for copying, pursuant to the provisions of said law, may be excluded therefrom by Executive Order of the Governor or by any regulation promulgated under the authority of any Executive Order of the Governor; and

WHEREAS, Section 3(e) of Executive Order No. 9, issued by Governor Richard Hughes in 1963, and reaffirmed by Executive Order No. 123, issued by Governor Thomas H. Kean in 1983, states that fingerprint cards, plates and photographs and other similar criminal investigation records which are required to be made, maintained or kept by any State or local governmental agency shall not be deemed to be public records subject to inspection and examination and available for copying pursuant to the provisions of Chapter 73; and

WHEREAS, the Attorney General has undertaken a complete review of this subject area, seeking input from prosecutors, police, representatives of the news media, and victims' rights organizations, and has recommended that certain aspects of the system be clarified;

NOW, THEREFORE, I, Christine Todd Whitman, Governor of the State of New Jersey, by virtue of the authority vested in me by the Constitution and by the Statutes of this State, do hereby order and direct:

Executive Order No. 9 of Governor Richard J. Hughes and Executive Order No. 123 of Governor Thomas H. Kean are modified as hereinafter set forth, and any regulations adopted and promulgated under those prior Executive Orders shall be deemed null and void to the extent such regulations are inconsistent with the provisions of this Executive Order.

The following records shall not be deemed to be public records subject to inspection and examination and available for copying pursuant to the provisions of Chapter 73, P.L. 1963, as amended: fingerprint cards, plates and photographs and similar criminal investigation records that are required to be made, maintained or kept by any State or local governmental agency.

Notwithstanding the above section 2, the following information shall be available to the public within 24 hours, or sooner if practicable, of a request for such information:

where a crime has been reported but no arrest yet made, information as to the type of crime, time, location and type of weapon, if any;

if an arrest has been made, information as to the name, address and age of any victims, unless there has not been sufficient opportunity for notification of next of kin of any victims of injury and/or death to any such victim or where the release of the names of any victim would be contrary to existing law or court rule. In deciding on the release of information as to the identity of a victim, the safety of the victim and the victim's family, and the integrity of any ongoing investigation, shall be considered;

if an arrest has been made, information as to the defendant's name, age, residence, occupation, marital status and similar background information and the identity of the complaining party, unless the release of such information is contrary to existing law or court rule;

information as to the text of any charges, such as the complaint, accusation and indictment, unless sealed by the court or unless the release of such information is contrary to existing law or court rule;

information as to the identity of the investigating and arresting personnel and agency and the length of the investigation;

information of the circumstances immediately surrounding the arrest, including but not limited to the time and place of the arrest, resistance, if any, pursuit, possession and nature and use of weapons and ammunition by the suspect and by the police; and

information as to circumstances surrounding bail, whether it was posted and amount thereof.

The term "request" shall mean either a written or oral request; provided, however, that all requests are made with sufficient clarity so as to enable a reasonable person to understand the information that is being sought. The law enforcement official responding to oral requests should make best efforts to respond orally over the telephone; however, it shall not be unreasonable to require the requester to appear in person to receive the information. Unless the parties note otherwise, it shall be understood that there is no duty to release or obtain information that is not in the possession of the law enforcement agency at the time of request.

Notwithstanding any other provision of this Executive Order, where it shall appear that the information requested or to be examined will jeopardize the safety of any person or jeopardize any investigation in progress or may be otherwise inappropriate to release, such information may be withheld. This section is intended to be narrowly construed to prevent disclosure of information which would be truly harmful to a bona fide law enforcement purpose or public safety if released. It is also intended to prevent such release that would violate existing law regarding confidentiality in areas including, but not limited to, domestic violence and juveniles.

Each county prosecutor shall prepare a plan outlining the procedures for providing and/or disseminating the information required by this Executive Order and shall submit same to the Division of Criminal Justice for its review and filing. Each prosecutor shall consult with the police departments within his or her county and to the extent possible, include within the prosecutor's plan the local procedures for responding to informational requests. The Division of State Police shall submit its plan to the Office of the Attorney General. Whenever any changes are made in any such plan, said changes shall immediately be forwarded to the appropriate county prosecutor and/or the Division of Criminal Justice or Office of the Attorney General for review and filing. In addition, each county prosecutor's office shall designate a person(s) who is(are) responsible for responding to requests for public information by the media on nights, weekends and holidays. The name of the person(s) so designated shall be available at the communication center in each county.

The Attorney General, as chief law enforcement officer of the State, or his designee, or where appropriate, the county prosecutor, as chief law enforcement officer of the county, shall promptly resolve all disputes as to whether or not the release of records would be "otherwise inappropriate" between the custodian of any records referred to herein and any person seeking access thereto or similar disputes. Where the Attorney General or the county prosecutor determines that the release of records would be "otherwise inappropriate," he or she shall issue a brief statement explaining the decision.

The terms of the Order shall be carried out in the spirit of Chapter 73, P.L. 1963, as amended, and shall not relate to requests pursuant to Chapter 60, Section 4, of P.L. 1994. It shall be carried out by keeping in mind the right of citizens to be aware of events occurring in their community.

This Order shall take effect immediately.

Once again, your state may have its own set of provisions or the local police department may post how you can get police reports in your area. Most often the only thing they'll need to ask you for is the money for the copies!

Chapter 7

Talking to the Police

Many of us may be unsure of what our rights are when we are not in custody. When you are in custody, well that's that easy. You have the right to remain silent...etc. Still you may be unaware that you do not have to answer the police when being questioned during a non-custodial interview. You don't have to speak with them when you are in custody outside of the presence of your lawyer either, but for the purposes of this discussion, here are some excellent guidelines as they are found at : **www.halcyon.com/elf/police.html**

Your Rights and the Police

What with Senators Exon and the rest of that rat-trap we call a Congress attempting to control what we say and do, I for one have no intention of pulling my material off the Internet anytime soon. With that in mind, I offer the following sound advice, offered up from my notes at a local ACLU seminar...

What you say to the police is important. It can be used against you, and it can give the police an excuse to arrest you, especially if you speak disrespectfully to a police officer.

You do not have to answer a police officer's questions. If you are stopped while driving a car, you must show your driver's license, registration, and proof of insurance. In other situations, you cannot be legally arrested for refusing to identify yourself.

You do not have to give your consent to any search of your person, your car, or your house; if you do consent to a search, it can affect your rights later in court. If the police claim they have a warrant, ask to see it. Whether or not the police have a warrant to search you or your property, you can protect your rights by making it clear that you do not agree to any search.

Do not interfere with, physically resist, or obstruct the police in a search, even if you are sure the search is illegal—you will be arrested for it. File a complaint afterwards if you feel your rights have been violated.

If confronted by a police officer, you may remain silent. You do not have to answer any questions, give your name, age, or address, or show any ID unless you are operating a car or are in a place where liquor is served. However, it is advisable to provide basic information such as name, age, and address.

Ask if you are under arrest. If so, ask why. If you are not under arrest, you should be free to leave. Insist on that right. *Never run from a police officer.*

Never physically resist. The police may frisk you for weapons by patting the outside of your clothing, but nothing more. Make it clear that you do not agree to any search. If you are searched, do not resist. File a complaint afterwards.

If you are stopped in your car, show your driver's license, registration, and proof of insurance upon request. Your car can be searched without a warrant so long as the officer has probable cause. To protect yourself, make it clean that you do not consent to a search. If given a ticket, sign it; you can be arrested for failing to do so. The proper place to fight a ticket is in court. Your license can be suspended if you refuse to take a breath test if you are stopped for suspected drunk driving.

If you are arrested, go with the officer. Do not resist. Do not answer the officer's questions. Whether or not you are guilty, do not resist arrest. You can make your defense in court. You have the right to remain silent; use it. Tell the police nothing except your name, age, and address. Don't give explanations or stories or try to excuse your conduct.

Ask to talk to a lawyer at once. You can do so by phone immediately after being taken into custody. If you are arrested for a jailable offense and you cannot afford a lawyer, you have the right to a public defender. Do not talk to the police until a lawyer is present.

If during a search or an arrest the police take anything from you, they must give you a receipt for every item seized, including your wallet and its contents, clothes, and any packages you were carrying when arrested.

You may be released with or without bail following the booking. If not, you have the right to go into court and see a judge the next *court* day after your arrest. Demand this right. When you appear before the judge, ask for an attorney.

Never make any decisions in your case until you have spoken with a lawyer.

This is not complete advice. Be sure to consult a legal professional.

Chapter 8

Public Records
How to Get Em',
How to Use Em'

As previously mentioned police records are generally a matter of public record and you have the right to obtain them. Many of these documents fall under our federal freedom of information acts passed by Congress. What this means is that you have a right to review these documents especially if you intend to use them in a criminal or civil proceeding against your opponent. Crime victims also have special rights and considerations even up to having the perpetrator reimburse them for damages.

How to Get Driving Records in Any State:

That withstanding, the law is quite favorable in assisting your access to such public records.

You also have several options for their procurement. For example, if you are considering litigation, (civil or criminal), for something involving damages suffered as the result of a car accident, you have the right to request copies of the defendant's driving records. Certified copies are available from Motor Vehicle Services in your state. If you live in New Jersey, here is the address to write to for a request form:

Motor Vehicle Services
Information & Systems Management
Data Output / Driver Abstract
P.O. Box 142
Trenton, NJ 08666-0142

Each state has a similar department which keeps track of each licensed driver's record. In addition to requesting a complete certified abstract, you can also request other separate documents. Other such reports include summons issued, surcharges and surcharge schedule,

license revocation, etc. The fees are nominal too. For a certified abstract, the fee is only $10.00. For certified related documents such as I've just mentioned, the fee is only $5.00 per report. Simply fill out the request form, include a photo copy of your *valid* driver's license, put in your check after selecting the documents you want and you're done.

You will be much better armed walking into court with this background information on your opponent than if you didn't bother trying to obtain them at all. Such powerful evidence is enough to impeach the testimony of your opponent, especially when he starts in with what a spotless driving record he has.

Another point to note is the courts look with great disfavor upon those who both lie and break the law. If your adversary was involved in an accident while driving while on the revoked or suspended list, well that is a whole new set of charges. If you don't believe how serious this is, I'd like you to turn your attention to Appendix II in the back of this book and look under New Jersey's Driving Violations as listed under "Foolish Life Mistake # 101, Driving while Suspended".

Each state has it's own system, but for the most part, your opponent will be in big trouble once it is has been found out that he's been flying around causing even more accidents while on the revoked list.

Now you can pay the cheaper fees as just listed from your local division of motor vehicles or you have the option of hiring a private investigator to get them for you. There are many on-line "snoops" ready to go digging for you and it is completely legal. Once again these are public records and if you have a legitimate reason for needing them, such as for court, you can access them. Things may change a little in the future as far as restrictions on who may and may not tap into this information but until then, it's an open arena. Bill Clinton's signing of the Privacy Act is perhaps the most significant challenge to date on your ability to view these documents.

How to Get Public Records in Any State:

For example, private investigators can provide you with the following information in just a few hours in some cases. Let's say you need the perpetrator's driving records in a matter of days and can't wait for your request to come back from your state's department of motor vehicles. Then you have one of these detective services do the search for you, but expect to pay quite a bit more than what your state office will charge. All the same if this information will make or break your case, it may well be worth spending the extra cash. The legal citation services that I mentioned in the beginning of this book such as Lexis and Westlaw also have public records files. Your attorney only needs the proper spelling of the defendant's last name to pull up the following documents:

- Assets
- Bankruptcy Records
- Real Estate Ownership Records
- Federal, State and County Liens
- Motor Vehicle Ownership
- Personal / Business Credit Reports
- Criminal Records
- Driving Records

There is even much more information than this listed under public records such as marine motor craft registrations and Dun and Bradstreet listings but I doubt if you'll find these of much use or interest. These searches of public records can be done on individuals or businesses if that's who you're taking to court. In any event, these are all part of a national registry as it were so no matter what state you live in, you have access to such public information.

Chapter 9

Appearing in Municipal Court and Reasons Why You Might Be There

For practically everyone, the first contact with the criminal justice system of your state will come by way of your appearance in municipal court. Traffic tickets, drunk driving, jay walking, its all there. All the same, having some knowledge of what actually goes on in municipal court and in what order may help you to make it through this stressful experience.

The following website is listed in the reference section as one of "the" five best reference websites on the web for New Jersey Municipal Court law. Although there may be minor differences state to state, their's is a very basic format which you will find is followed by most every other local court in the country. Penalties and laws may vary, but for the most part, no matter where you live, this is what you can expect. Be sure to visit them on-line to view all of their documents. A wonderful resource!

Here's an excellent printout from: **www.municipalcourt.com**

The Municipal Court desires that you receive a full and fair hearing. In order to do so you should be aware of the following facts:

1. You are presumed to be innocent until proven guilty beyond a reasonable doubt.
2. You have the right to be represented by an attorney.
3. You have the right to be assigned an attorney if:

(a) You are charged with a non-indictable offense and the Judge determines you cannot afford an attorney or

(b) You are charged with a non-indictable offense and the Judge determines you cannot afford an attorney and there is a likelihood that if you are convicted you will either go to jail, receive a substantial fine or your driver's license will be suspended.

4. You have the right to obtain a postponement for a good cause, or to obtain legal counsel and prepare a proper defense.

5. You have the right to call witnesses or have them ordered to appear by the court.6. You have the right to plead guilty or not guilty to any charge against you.

7. If you are charged with an indictable offense, the Judge cannot ask for your plea because you have the right to a probable cause hearing before the Judge and a trial by jury at the county level if the Grand Jury indicts.

8. There are, however, certain indictable offenses that may be tried by the Judge if you waive indictment and trial by jury in writing. You have the right to be informed if you have been charged with such an offense.

9. When your case is called, please come forward quickly and quietly. You will then have the charges read to you and you may plead "guilty" or "not guilty".

10. This is not the time to tell your story. You will be given an opportunity to do so at a later time in the proceedings. The only purpose of asking you to plead guilty or not guilty is to determine whether you want a trial and have the judge decide whether you violated the law as charged. If you are in doubt enter a plea of "not guilty".

11. What happens when you plead guilty? When you plead guilty, it is not necessary to have a trial. You have admitted that you violated the law and all that remains is for the Judge to fix the penalty. The arresting officer or other complainant will explain briefly the circumstances of the violation and you may then explain to the court any extenuating circumstances. The Judge will then assess the penalty.

12. If you plead not guilty, you and the witnesses will be placed under oath to speak the truth. It is necessary for the prosecution to prove the charges

made against you before it is necessary for you to answer these charges. You, or your counsel, have the right to ask the prosecutor's witnesses any questions pertaining to the charges.

13. When the prosecution has finished, you may then present your own witnesses; or testify in your own behalf. You are not forced to testify against yourself, but you may testify, if you so desire. Any evidence you give may be used by either side. If you do testify, the prosecution then has the right to ask you any questions concerning the charges.

14. When all the witnesses have testified, you or your attorney may tell this court why you think you should not be found guilty.

15. If the court finds you guilty, and you think the court is in error, you have ten (10) days within which to appeal. Appeals in practically all instances will be heard by the County Court.

16. Damages growing out of a collision cannot be adjudicated by this court. This court is only concerned with violations of the State statutes and municipal ordinances. Damages are a civil matter and will have to be tried in a civil court.

17. While it is the constant endeavor of the municipality and the Judge to see that no advantage is taken of your unfamiliarity with these matters, they cannot be expected to serve as your legal counsel.

18. Every person has the right to make his own defense without counsel, but if you are in doubt as to the proper course, it is recommended that you consult an attorney.

19. Cases usually will be heard in this order:
    (1) application for adjournments
    (2) guilty pleas
    (3) contested matters with an attorney
    (4) other contested matters.

20. If you come to court for a traffic offense, and you have not previously notified the court of your intention to plead "not guilty", speak to the court clerk immediately. If the officer or others involved can be contacted to testify, your case may be heard. If they cannot be reached, you will have

to make another court appearance at a later date. If you follow these suggestions, your case can be handled more efficiently.

Epiloge

I hope this book has offered you some comfort if you have been facing similar problems with your local court or police department. What you don't know can hurt you as it puts you at a serious disadvantage legally. Therefore forewarned is forearmed.

My story obviously appears to be an unfinished account. So many questions remain unanswered such as...

Will Hattie and her cohorts get their just desserts for lying?
Will Judge Thuman be thrown off the bench?
Will the ditzy court administrator Fatima B. Wombat be fired?
Will all of these people end up being indicted on Federal conspiracy charges?

We shall see in the sequel to this book!

Appendix I
New Jersey's Traffic Laws

Life's Mistake # 100), (Not One of Mine!)

Driving Without Insurance. If you live in New Jersey or any other state that requires that drivers carry insurance, don't even think about doing this. He's New Jersey's rules on the books as it appears at-**www.municipal-court.com**:

B-2. Violations; punishment. Any owner or registrant of a motor vehicle registered or principally garaged in this state who operates or causes to be operated a motor vehicle upon any public road or highway in this state without motor vehicle liability insurance coverage required by this act, and any operator who operates or causes a motor vehicle to be operated and who knows or should know from the attendant circumstances that the motor vehicle is without motor vehicle liability insurance coverage required by this act [chapter] shall be subject, for the first offense, to a fine of $300.00 and a period of community service to be determined by the court, and shall forthwith forfeit his right to operate a motor vehicle over the highways of this state for a period of one year from the date of conviction.

Upon subsequent conviction, he shall be subject to a fine of $500.00 and shall be subject to imprisonment for a term of 14 days and shall be ordered by the court to perform community service for a period of 30 days, which shall be of such form and on such terms as the court shall deem appropriate under the circumstances, and shall forfeit his right to operate a motor vehicle for a period of 2 years from the date of his conviction, and, after the expiration of said period, he may make application to the director of the division of motor vehicles for a license to operate a motor vehicle, which application may be granted at the discretion of the director. The director's discretion shall be based upon an assessment of the motor vehicle to be operated in the future without the insurance coverage required by this act [chapter] A complaint for violation of this act [chapter] may be months after the date of the alleged offense.

Failure to produce at the time of trial an insurance identification card or an insurance policy which was in force for the time of operation for which the offense is charged, creates a rebuttable presumption that the person was uninsured when charged with the violation of this section.

Notwithstanding any provision of P.L. 1972. c. 197 (C. 39:6B-1 et seq.) any person who violates the provisions of that act, from October 1, 1990 through January 31, 1991, shall not be subject to any of the penalties or sanctions provided for a first violation of that act if that person produces at the time of trial an insurance identification card or a motor vehicle liability insurance policy which is in force at the time of the trial and the conviction for that person's offense would be their first conviction for an offense under that act. The Commissioner of Insurance shall appropriately promote and advertise this limited time amnesty program for first-time offenses under that act throughout the State.

Appendix II
New Jersey's Driving Violations

Foolish Life Mistake # 101, (Also Not One of Mine!)

Driving While Suspended

39:3-40. Driving when license refused, suspended, revoked or prohibited; motor vehicle license revoked; punishment. No person to whom a driver's license has been refused or whose driver's license or reciprocity privilege has been suspended or revoked, or who has been prohibited from obtaining a driver's license, shall personally operate a motor vehicle during the period of refusal, suspension, revocation, or prohibition.

No person whose motor vehicle registration has been revoked shall operate or permit the operation of such motor vehicle during the period of such revocation.

A person violating this section shall be subject to the following penalties:

   a. Upon conviction for a first offense, a fine of $500.00;

   b. Upon conviction for a second offense, a fine of $750.00 and imprisonment in the county jail for not more then 5 days;

   c. Upon conviction for a third offense, a fine of $1,000.00 and imprisonment in the county jail for 10 days;

   d. Upon conviction, the court shall impose or extend a period of suspension not to exceed six months;

   e. Upon conviction, the court shall impose a period of imprisonment for not less than 45 days, if while operating a vehicle in violation of this section a person is involved in an accident resulting in personal injury to another person.

f. Notwithstanding subsections a. through e., any person violating this section while under suspension issued pursuant to R.S. 39:4-50 or section 2 of P.L. 1972, c.197 (C.39:6B-2) upon conviction, shall be fined $500.00, shall have his license to operate a motor vehicle suspended for an additional period of not less than one year nor more than two years, and may be imprisoned in the county jail for not more than 90 days.

g. In addition to the other applicable penalties provided under this section, a person violating this section whose license has been suspended pursuant to section 6 of P.L 1983, c.65 (C. 17:29A-35) or the regulations adopted thereunder, shall be fined $3,000. The court shall waive the fine upon proof that the person has paid the total surcharge imposed pursuant to section 6 of P.L. 1983, c.65 (C.17:29A-35) or the regulations adopted thereunder, Notwithstanding the provisions of R.S. 39:5-41, the fine imposed pursuant to this subsection shall be collected by the Division of Motor Vehicles pursuant to section 6 of P.L. 1983, c.65 (C.17:29A-35), and distributed as provided in that section, and the court shall file a copy of the judgment of conviction with the director and with the Clerk of the Superior Court who shall enter the following information upon the record of docketed judgments: the name of the person as judgment debtor; the Division of Motor Vehicles as judgment creditor; the amount of the fine; and the date of the order. These entries shall have the same force and effect as any civil judgment docketed in the Superior Court.

Idiotic Life Mistake # 102-103, (Definitely Not Any of Mine Either)

Driving While Intoxicated

39:4-49.1. Operating with drugs in possession or in motor vehicle; penalty:
No person shall operate a motor vehicle on any highway while knowingly having in his possession or in the motor vehicle on any highway while knowingly having in his possession or in the motor vehicle any controlled dangerous substance as classified in Schedules I, II, III, IV, and V of the "New Jersey Controlled Dangerous Substances Act, "P.L. 1970, c. 226 (C. 24:21 et seq.) or any prescription legend drug, unless the person has obtained the substance or drug from, or on a valid written prescription of, a duty licensed physician, veterinarian, dentist or other medical practitioner licensed to write prescriptions intended for the treatment or prevention of disease in man or animals or unless the person possesses a controlled dangerous substance pursuant to a lawful order of a practitioner or lawfully possesses a Schedule V substance.

A person who violates this section shall be fined not less than $50.00 and shall forthwith forfeit his right to operate a motor vehicle for a period of 2 years from the date of his conviction.

39:4-49.2. Section inapplicable to certain persons.
The provisions of section 1 [39:4-49.1] of this act shall not apply to a duly licensed physician, dentist, registered pharmacist, veterinarian, nurse, podiatrist, intern or resident physician of a hospital, sanitarium or other medical institution; or to a hospital, sanitarium, clinical laboratory or any other medical institution; or to a state or governmental agency; or to any manufacturer, wholesaler, retailer or regular dealer in drugs.

39:4-49.3. Additional exceptions.

The provisions of section 1 [39:4-49.1] of this act shall not apply to common carriers or to warehousemen while engaged in lawfully transporting or storing such drugs or to any employee of the same acting within the scope of his employment; or to public officers or employees in the performance of their official duties requiring possession or control of these drugs; or to temporary incidental possession by employees or agents of persons lawfully entitled to possession; or to persons whose possession is for the purpose of aiding public officers in performing their official duties.

39:4-50. Operating under influence of liquor or drugs; penalty; forfeiture of right to operate; rehabilitation programs.

(a) A person who operates a motor vehicle while under the influence of intoxicating liquor, narcotic, hallucinogenic or habit producing drug, or operates a motor vehicle with a blood alcohol concentration of 0.10% or more by weight of alcohol in the defendant's blood or permits another person who is under the influence of intoxicating liquor, narcotic, hallucinogenic or habit producing drug to operate a motor vehicle owned by him or in his custody or control or permits another to operate a motor vehicle with a blood alcohol concentration of 0.10% or more by weight of alcohol in the defendant's blood, shall be subject:

(1) For the first offense, to a fine of not less than $250.00 nor more than $400.00 and a period of detainment of not less than 12 hours nor more than 48 hours spent during two consecutive days of not less than six hours each day and served as prescribed by the program requirements of the Intoxicated Driver Resource Centers established under subsections (1) of this section and, in the discretion of the court, a team of imprisonment of not more than 30 days and shall forthwith forfeit his right to operate a motor vehicle over the highways of this State for a period of not less than six months nor more than one year.

(2) For a second violation, a person shall be subject to a fine of not less than $500.00 nor more than $1,000.00 and shall be ordered by the court to perform community service for a period of 30 days, which shall

be of such form and on such terms as the court shall deem appropriate under the circumstances, and shall be sentenced to imprisonment for a term of not less than 48 consecutive hours, which shall not be suspended or served on probation, nor more than 90 days, and shall forfeit his right to operate a motor vehicle over the highways of this State for a period of two years upon conviction, and after the expiration of said period, he may make application to the Director of the Division of Motor Vehicles for a license to operate a motor vehicle, which application may be granted at the discretion of the director, consistent with subsection (b) of this section.

(3) For a third or subsequent violation, a person shall be subject to a fine of $1,000.00, and shall be sentenced to imprisonment for a term of not less than 180 days, except that the court may lower such term for each day, not exceeding 90 days, served performing community service in such form and on such terms as the court shall deem appropriate under the circumstances and shall thereafter forfeit his rights to operate a motor vehicle over the highways of this State for 10 years.

Whenever an operator of a motor vehicle has been involved in an accident resulting in death, bodily injury or property damage, a police officer shall consider that fact along with all other facts and circumstances in determining whether there are reasonable grounds to believe that person was operating a motor vehicle in violation of this section.

If the driving privilege of any person is under revocation or suspension for a violation of any provision of this Title or Title 2C of the New Jersey Statutes at the time of any conviction for a violation of this section, the revocation or suspension period imposed shall commence as the date of termination of the existing revocation or suspension period. In the case of any person who at the time of the imposition of sentence is less than 17 years of age, the forfeiture, suspension or revocation of the driving privilege imposed by the court under this section shall commence immediately, run through the offender's seventeenth birthday and continue from the date for the period set by the court pursuant to paragraphs (1) through (3) of this subsection.

A court that imposes a term of imprisonment under this section may sentence the person so convicted to the county jail, to the workhouse of the county wherein the offense was committed, to an inpatient rehabilitation program or to an Intoxicated Driver Resource Center or other facility approved by the chief of the Intoxicated Driving Program Unit in the Department of Health; provided that for a third or subsequent offense a person shall not serve a term of imprisonment at an Intoxicated Driver Resource Center as provided in subsection (f).

A person who has been convicted of a previous violation of this section need not be charged as a second or subsequent offender in the compliant made against him in order to render him liable to the punishment imposed by this section on a second or subsequent offender, but if the second offense occurs more than 10 years after the first offense, the court shall treat the second conviction as a first offense for sentencing purposes and if a third offense occurs more than 10 years after the second offense occurs more than 10 years after the second offense, the court shall treat the third conviction as a second offense for sentencing purposes.

(b) A person convicted under this section must satisfy the screening, evaluation, referral, program and fee requirements of the Division of Alcoholism and Drug Abuse Intoxicated Driving Program Unit, and of the Intoxicated Driver Resource Centers and a program of alcohol education and highway safety, as prescribed by the Director of the Division of Motor Vehicles. The sentencing court shall inform the person convicted that failure to satisfy such requirements shall result in a mandatory two day term of imprisonment in a county jail and a driver license revocation or suspension and continuation of revocation or suspension until such requirements are satisfied, unless stayed by court order in accordance with Rule 7:8-2 of the Rules Governing the Courts of the State of New Jersey, or R.S. 39:5-22. Upon sentencing, the court shall forward to the Bureau of Alcohol Countermeasures within the Intoxicated Driving Program Unit a copy of a person's conviction record. A fee of $100.00 shall be payable to the Alcohol Education, Rehabilitation and

Enforcement Fund established pursuant to section 3 of P.L. 1983, c. 531 (C. 26:2B-32) to support the Intoxicated Driving Program Unit.

(c) Upon conviction of a violation of this section, the court shall collect forthwith the New Jersey driver's license or licenses of the person so convicted and forward such license or licenses to the Director of the Division of Motor Vehicles. The court shall inform the person convicted that if he is convicted of personally operating a motor vehicle during the period of license suspension imposed pursuant to subsection (a) of this section, he shall, upon conviction, be subject to the penalties established in R.S. 39:3-40. The person convicted shall be informed orally and in writing. A person shall be required to acknowledge receipt of that written notice in writing. Failure to receive a written notice or failure to acknowledge in writing the receipt of a written notice shall not be a defense to a subsequent charge of a violation of R.S. 39:3-40.

In the event that a person convicted under this section is the holder of any out-of-state driver's license, the court shall not collect the license but shall notify forthwith the director, who shall, in turn, notify appropriate officials in the licensing jurisdiction. The court shall, however, revoke the nonresident's driving privilege to operate a motor vehicle in this State, in accordance with this section. Upon conviction of a violation of this section, the court shall notify the person convicted, orally and in writing, of the penalties for a second, third or subsequent violation of this section. A person shall be required to acknowledge receipt of that written notice in writing. Failure to receive a written notice or failure to acknowledge in writing the receipt of a written notice shall not be a defense to a subsequent charge of a violation of this section.

(d) The Director of the Division of Motor Vehicles shall promulgate rules and regulations pursuant to the "Administrative Procedure Act," P.L. 1968, c.410 (C. 52:14B-1 et seq.) in order to establish a program of alcohol education and highway safety, as prescribed by this act.

(e) Any person accused of a violation of this section who is liable to punishment imposed by this section as a second or subsequent offender shall be entitled to the same rights of discovery as allowed defendants pursuant to the Rules Governing Criminal Practice, as set forth in the Rules Governing the Courts of the State of New Jersey.

(f) The counties, in cooperation with the Division of Alcoholism and Drug Abuse and the Division of Motor Vehicles, but subject to the approval of the Division of Alcoholism and Drug Abuse, shall designate and establish on a county or regional basis Intoxicated Driver Resource Centers. These centers shall have the capability of serving as community treatment referral centers and as court monitors of a person's compliance with the ordered treatment, service alternative or community service. All centers established pursuant to this subsection shall be administered by a certified alcoholism counselor or other professional with a minimum of five years' experience in the treatment of alcoholism.

All centers shall be required to develop individualized treatment plans for all persons attending the centers; provided that the duration of any ordered treatment or referral shall not exceed one year. It shall be the center's responsibility to establish networks with the community alcohol education, treatment and rehabilitation resources and to receive monthly reports from the referral agencies regarding a person's participation and compliance with the program. Nothing in this subsection shall bar these centers from developing their own education and treatment programs; provided that they are approved by the Division of Alcoholism and Drug Abuse.

Upon a person's failure to report to the initial screening or any subsequent ordered referral, the Intoxicated Driver Resource Center shall promptly notify the sentencing court of the person's failure to comply.

Required detention periods at the Intoxicated Driver Resource Centers shall be determined according to the individual treatment classification assigned by the Bureau of Alcohol Countermeasures. Upon attendance at an Intoxicated Driver Resource Center, a person shall be required to pay a per diem fee of $75.00 for the first offender program or a per diem fee of $100.00 for the second offender program, as appropriate, Any increases in the per diem fees after the first full year shall be determined pursuant to rules and regulations adopted by the Commissioner of Health in consultation with the

Governor's Council on Alcoholism and Drug Abuse pursuant to the "Administrative Procedure Act," P.L. 1968, c.410 (C. 52:14B-1 et seq.).

The centers shall conduct a program of alcohol education and highway safety, as prescribed by the Director of the Division of Motor Vehicles.

The commissioner of Health shall adopt rules and regulations pursuant to the "Administrative Procedure Act," P.L. 1968, c.410 (C. 52:14B-1 et seq.) in order to effectuate the purposes of this subsection.

"DWI Refusal"
(This is Life's Idiotic Mistake # 104 In Case You're Wondering)
39:4-50.4a. Revocation of license for refusal to submit to chemical tests.

The municipal court shall revoke the right to operate a motor vehicle of any operator who, after being arrested for a violation of R.S. 39:4-50, shall refuse to submit a test provided for in section 2 of P.L. 1966, c. 142 (C. 39:4-50.2) when requested to do so, for six months unless the refusal was in connection with a second offense under this section, in which case the revocation period shall be for two years or unless the refusal was in connection with a third or subsequent offense under this section, in which case the revocation shall be for 10 years.

The municipal court shall determine by a preponderance of the evidence whether the arresting officer had probable cause to believe that the person had been driving or was in actual physical control of a motor vehicle on the public highways or quasi-public areas of this State while the person was under the influence of intoxicating liquor or a narcotic, hallucinogenic, or habit-producing drug or marihuana; whether the person was placed under arrest, if appropriate; and whether he refused to submit to the test upon request of the officer; and if these elements of the violation are not established, no conviction shall issue.

In addition to any other requirements provided by law, a person whose operator's license is revoked for refusing to submit to a test shall be referred to an Intoxicated Driver Resource Center established by subsection (f) of R.S.39:4-50 and shall satisfy the same requirements of the center for refusal to submit to a test as provided for in section 2 of P.L. 1966, c.142 (C.39.4-50.2) in connection with a first, second, third or subsequent offense under this section that must be satisfied by a person convicted of a commensurate violation of this section, or be subject to the same penalties as such a person for failure to do so. The revocation shall be independent of any revocation imposed by virtue of a conviction under the provisions of R.S. 39:4-50.

In addition to issuing a revocation, the municipal court shall fine a person convicted under this section, a fine of not less than $250.00 nor more than $500.00.

Life's Bone-headed Mistake # 105 (No Comment):

Speeding

39:4-95. "Vehicle" defined. As used in this article, the word "vehicle" includes street cars.

39:4-96. Reckless driving; punishment. A person who drives a vehicle heedlessly, in willful or wanton disregard of the rights or safety of others, in a manner so as to endanger, or be likely to endanger, a person or property, shall be guilty of reckless driving and be punished by imprisonment in the county or municipal jail for a period of not more than 60 days, or by a fine of not less than $40.00 or more than $200.00, or both.

On a second or subsequent conviction he shall be punished by imprisonment for not more than three months, or by a fine of not less than $100 or more than $500, or both.

39:4-97. Careless driving. A person who drives a vehicle carelessly, or without due caution and circumspection, in a manner so as to endanger, or be likely to endanger, a person or property, shall be guilty of careless driving.

39:4-98. Rates of speed. Subject to the provisions of sections 39:4-96 and 39:4-97 of this Title and except in those instances where a lower speed is specified in this chapter, it shall be prima facie lawful for the driver of a vehicle to drive it at a speed not exceeding the following:

a. Twenty-five miles an hour, when passing through a school zone during recess, when the presence of children is clearly visible from the roadway, or while children are going to or leaving school, during opening or closing hours;

b. (1) Twenty-five miles an hour in any suburban business or residential district;

(2) Thirty-five miles an hour in any suburban business or residential district;

c. Fifty miles an hour in all other locations.

Whenever it shall be determined upon the basis of an engineering and traffic investigation that any speed hereinbefore set forth is greater or less than is reasonable or safe under the conditions found to exist at any intersection or other place or upon any part of a highway, the commissioner of Transportation, with reference of State highways, may by regulation and municipal or county authorities, with reference to highways under their jurisdiction, may by ordinance, in the case of municipal authorities, or by ordinance or resolution, in the case of county authorities, subject to the approval of the Commissioner of Transportation, except as otherwise provided in R.S. 39:4-8, designate a reasonable and safe speed limit thereat which, subject to the provisions of R.S.30:4-96 and R.S. 39:4-97, shall be prima facie lawful at all times or at such times as may be determined, when appropriate signs giving notice thereof are erected at such intersection, or other place or part of the highway.

Appropriate signs giving notice of the speed limits authorized under the provisions of paragraph (1) of subsection b. and subsection c. of this section may be erected if the commissioner or the municipal or county authorities, as the case may be, so determine they are necessary. Appropriate signs giving notice of the speed limits authorized under the provisions of subsection a. and paragraph (2) of subsection b. of this section shall be erected by the commissioner or the municipal or county authorities, as appropriate.

The driver of every vehicle shall, consistent with the requirements of this section, drive at an appropriate reduced speed when approaching and crossing an intersection or railway grade crossing, when approaching and going around a curve, when narrow or winding roadway, and when special hazard exists with respect to pedestrians or other traffic or by reason of weather or highway conditions.

The Commissioner of Transportation shall cause the erection and maintenance of signs at such points of entrance to the State as are deemed advisable, setting forth the lawful rates of speed, the wording of which shall be within his discretion.

Appendix III
New Jersey State Driving Penalties, Surcharges & Point System

Penalties For Your Sins...

The New Jersey Merit Rating Plan, created by N.J.S.A. 17:29A-35, requires New Jersey Motor Vehicle Services to collect insurance surcharges from motorists whose driving records include certain motor vehicle offenses.

The bulk of the money collected is used to help in providing coverage for motorists who cannot obtain insurance on the open or voluntary market.

The surcharges are in addition to any court-imposed fines and penalties; or any premium/surcharge fees assessed by insurance companies.

Notice Of Proposed Suspension

If you are surcharged, the bill you receive is also an official Notice of Proposed Suspension of your driving privileges. The surcharge payments are due in full by the date printed on the bill. If you fail to pay the surcharge by the payment due date, your driving privileges will be indefinitely suspended. You will then have to pay a $50.00 restoration fee in addition to the full surcharge payment before your driving privileges can be restored.

If your license is already suspended for some other reason, and if you are suspended for failing to pay a surcharge, you must satisfy all suspensions before being restored.

Surchargeable Events Alcohol and Drug Related Offenses
Events Occurring on or after:

February 10, 1983	In-State "Operating Under the Influence of Liquor or Drugs" (DWI) violations
January 26, 1984	Out-of-State DWI violations
January 26, 1984	All "Refusal to submit to Chemical Test" violations

The surcharge for a drunk driving violation or refusal, whether occurring in New Jersey or another state, $1000 a year for three years for both a first and a second violation. A surcharge of $1,500 for three years will be imposed for a third or subsequent violation which occurs within three years of the first violation. If you are convicted of both a drunk driving and a refusal violation resulting from the same arrest, only one of the convictions will be surcharged.

Point Violations
(Occurring on or after February 10, 1983)

If you accumulate six or more points in a period of three calendar years or less you must pay an insurance surcharge of $100 for the first six points and $25 for each additional point. The point surcharge will remain in effect as long as you have six or more points on your record resulting from violations committed in the immediately preceding three-year calendar period.

Point Assessment Example:

If you accumulate two points in 1988 and two more in 1989 and an additional two in 1990, you would be subject to a $100 surcharge payment in 1991, since your record totals six points for the immediately preceding three calendar years. However, if you do not incur any additional point violations in 1991, you will not be surcharged in 1992, since your record for the immediately preceding three calendar years is now only four points (two points in 1989, two points in 1990, and zero points in 1991).

POINT REDUCTIONS ISSUED FOR ONE YEAR OF VIOLATION OR SUSPENSION—FREE DRIVING OR FOR COMPLETION OF A DRIVER IMPROVEMENT SCHOOL OR DEFENSIVE DRIVING COURSE ARE NOT CONSIDERED IN REVIEWING THE THREE-YEAR RECORD FOR SUR-CHARGE PURPOSES.

Your bill may include a "CATCH-UP" assessment if all surchargeable offenses were not recorded on your driving record at the time of your previous billing. If applicable, this will be noted on your bill.

OTHER SURCHARGEABLE EVENTS

(Regulation N.J.A.C. 13:19-13.1 ET SEQ)

Events occurring on or after March 19, 1984

Yearly Assessment*

Unlicensed Driver	$100
Driving While Suspended Court or DMV Reported	$250
No Liability Insurance on Motor Vehicle	$250

*These surcharges are assessed each year for three years.

References

Blacks Law Dictionary, Seventh Edition, West Group

Criminal Law 1999-00 Ed., Emanuel Publishing

Criminal Law, Cases and Materials, Kaplan & Weisberg, Little, Brown & Co.

Crimianl Law Handbook, Bergman and Barrett, Nolo Press—1999

Criminal Law & Procedure, Cases & Materials, 8 Ed., Boyce & Perkins, University Casebook Series

Criminal Procedure 1999-00 Ed., Emanuel Publishing

Everybody's Guide to Small Claims Court, Nolo Press—1998

Family Lawyer 2000, CD-ROM, Quicken

Lexis-Nexis Legal Internet Citation Service, Lexis Publishing

Neighbor Law, C. Jordan, Nolo Press-1998

New Jesery Court Rules State and Federal 2000, West Group

Represent Yourself in Court, Nolo Press—1998

Torts, Sum & Substance, 3d Ed., West Group

WestLaw on the Web, Legal Internet Citation Service, West Group

"The" Five Best Reference Websites on the Internet:

Federal Bureau of Investigation: **www.fbi.gov**

Municpal Court Information: **www.municipalcourt.com**

New Jersey Judiciary: **www.judiciary.state.nj.us**

U.S. Department of Justice: **www.usdoj.gov**

U.S. Law Website, "Ask a Lawyer": **www.uslaw.com**

www.ingramcontent.com/pod-product-compliance
Lightning Source LLC
Chambersburg PA
CBHW020248290526
45784CB00003B/1150